Journal of Interpretation

RID Publications
Registry of Interpreters for the Deaf, Inc.
8630 Fenton Street, Suite 324, Silver Spring, MD 20910, USA

The *Journal of Interpretation*, a publication of the Registry of Interpreters for the Deaf, Inc., publishes articles, research reports, and commentaries. The journal reflects a broad, interdisciplinary approach to the interpretation and translation of languages. The journal expressly desires to serve as a forum for the cross-fertilization of ideas from diverse theoretical and applied fields, examining signed or spoken language interpretation and translation.

American Psychological Association (APA) format for style, notes, and references is required for editorial consideration. Manuscripts may be submitted to the RID National Office, 8630 Fenton Street, Suite 324, Silver Spring, MD 20910. Submissions should be on computer disk. Three hard copies on 8 1/2 x 11 inch paper is requested to accompany the computer disk. Only files on 3 1/2 inch disks (Macintosh and Windows) are acceptable.

Editor: Douglas Watson, Ph.D.

RID Publications is a division of the Registry of Interpreters for the Deaf, Inc., 8630 Fenton Street, Suite 324, Silver Spring, MD 20910, USA, 301/608-0050 - v/tty

Internet: www.rid.org

Articles and reviews contained in the *Journal of Interpretation* do not necessarily reflect the official position of the Registry of Interpreters for the Deaf, Inc.

ISBN 0-916883-26-4

RID National Board of Directors

Daniel D. Burch, CSC
President

Ben Hall, CSC, Prov. SC:L
Vice President

Pam Brodie, CSC
Member-at-Large

Richard Laurion, IC/TC, CI and CT
Secretary/Treasurer

Hartmut Teuber, RSC
Region I Representative

Sue Scott, CSC, CI and CT
Region II Representative

Judith Lee Carson, CSC
Region III Representative

Linda Stauffer, CSC
Region IV Representative

Angela Jones, CI and CT
Region V Representative

Editor's Preface

It is a pleasure and honor to assume the role of editor and collaborate with the board and membership of RID to bring you the *Journal of Interpretation*. Through the editor's preface in each issue, I look forward to the opportunity to communicate with the journal's readership.

The process of producing a professional journal is a complex one, and perhaps what is most important is that it requires the cooperation and commitment of many. We would like to have an "open door" policy in which all our readers will have the opportunity to provide input by submitting manuscripts for publication, serving as peer reviewers, and writing book reviews. Your active participation is key to nurturing the success of the *JOI*.

A journal is as much a product of relationships as it is of ink and paper. The authors and their subjects, the panel of peer reviewers and referees, and the editors will all need to work together to produce a product of the quality expected by the readers and the profession. You, as the readers and subscribers, have a lot to say and much to contribute. It is *your* journal. We are here to work and collaborate with you to make it a journal that publishes high quality, timely articles. Our goal is to provide a communication network where ideas for improving research and practice in the field of interpretation can be expressed and exchanged.

This issue contains six articles on an assortment of topics: five are original manuscripts and one is a reprint. The article by Erik Peper and Katherine Gibney reports on the psychophysiological basis for discomfort during interpreting; Christopher Haas writes about the relationship between the interpreting process and memory or recall; Jack Hoza discusses "saving face" in the interpreting situation; Carolyn Ressler provides a comparative analysis of a direct interpretation and relay interpretation of ASL; and the paper by Linda Stauffer, Daniel Burch, and Steven Boone outlines the demographic profile from a sample of participants at the 1997 RID Convention. Holly Mikkelson, of the Monterey Institute of International Studies, graciously permitted *JOI* to reprint an article she had published previously for the general field about the professionalization of community interpreting. These articles share a common theme: a search to identify and understand underlying processes that can be harnessed to improve and otherwise enhance teaching, research, and practice by the interpreting profession.

I would like to especially acknowledge and thank the team of reviewers who played such an important role in the editorial process. Upon taking office as the Editor for *JOI*, and faced with the immediate mandate to solicit, select, and edit manuscripts suitable for publication, I assembled a "panel of reviewers" to assist me in the task. They have done more than their fair share, as each member spent literally hours going over manuscripts and making suggestions or comments that were helpful and assistive to authors and the editor. My belief that journal writing is an educational process has been reflected by the work of the reviewers. These reviewers approached manuscripts more in terms of how they could be improved, rather than only how to reject. Members of the "panel of reviewers" for this issue of *JOI* included Steven Boone, Heidi LeFebure, Susan McGee, Myra Taff-Watson, Kathy Wheeler-Scruggs, and Sherman Wilcox. They deserve recognition for their excellent work in assisting in the selection and editing of the manuscripts in this issue.

Finally, I would like to share with the readership that we are accepting nominations for individuals who might have the skills and interest needed to serve as peer reviewers and editors for the *JOI*. We would like to organize a pool of 25-30 individuals who have a variety of backgrounds and experience in the field to serve on the new *JOI* Board of Editors and Peer Review Panels that we plan to establish. A Board of Editors will comprise the "senior pool of peer reviewers" who will serve three to five-year terms of office. The Peer Reviewers will be composed of individuals with special expertise who are currently willing to review in their area of expertise as needed and have an interest in serving as future Board of Editors members. If you would like to nominate an individual or volunteer your services for either of these roles, please contact the RID National Office.

Douglas Watson
Editor
Little Rock, Arkansas
DWatson@comp.uark.edu

Contents

Journal of Interpretation

Psychophysiological Basis for Discomfort During Sign Language Interpreting

Erik Peper and Katherine Hughes Gibney
San Francisco State University

Psychophysiological Basis for Discomfort During Sign Language Interpreting[1,2]

Erik Peper and Katherine Hughes Gibney
San Francisco State University[3]

"I had no idea I began breathing so quickly when I interpreted."
—SFSU interpreter

Abstract

Professional sign language interpreters are an essential link to the speaking world for millions of deaf and hard of hearing Americans. These interpreters report a greater than 50% incidence of discomfort and pain in wrists, elbows, shoulders, and back. This study explored the psychophysiological correlates associated with sign language interpreting. Subjects were nine professional sign language interpreters. Respiration, peripheral temperature, skin conductance, and surface electromyography (sEMG) from upper trapezius and forearm were recorded during pre-baseline, 15 minutes of interpreting and post-baseline. During interpreting the mean respiration rate increased by 70%; mean hand temperature decreased from 73.9° to 70.8°F; mean skin conductance increased by 50%; and sEMG increased. Subjects were unaware of their physiological changes. This psychophysiological profile (a state of high arousal) can contribute to the development and continuation of discomfort associated with repetitive motion injury (RMI). To reduce the risk of injury, interpreters need to learn diaphragmatic breathing, hand warming, and brief muscular rest periods as well as integrate these skills during interpreting.

Sign language is an integral form of communication for millions of Americans with hearing impairments. It ranks as the fourth most common language in the United States. Although individuals who are deaf or hard of hearing communicate amongst one another fairly easily using sign language, they depend upon hearing individuals who also communicate in sign language to interpret the spoken word into sign language. In more formal environments (e.g., schools, medical settings, courtrooms) interpretation and/or transliteration usually is provided by trained professional sign language interpreters. These interpreters report a very high incidence of discomfort and pain, especially in the wrists, elbows, shoulders and back. These symptoms are commonly described as repetitive motion injuries (RMIs) and can include such diagnoses as tendonitis and carpal tunnel syndrome. RMIs are on the rise and becoming a very serious problem among professional inter-preters. The National Technical Institute for the Deaf (DeCaro, Feuerstein, & Hurwitz, 1992) indicated that 45% of their inter-preters were either totally disabled or were interpreting fewer hours due to pain. At San Francisco State University (SFSU) approximately 4% of the interpreters per year file Workers' Compensation claims. It is important to note that most individuals who are deaf and communicate in sign language do not report sim-ilar symptoms even though they perform similar hand, wrist, elbow, arm, and shoulder movements as the interpreters.

There appears to be a similarity of symptomology reported by professional interpreters and those who work at computers (Peper, Wilson, Taylor, Pierce, Bender, & Tibbetts, 1994). Both jobs require repetitive motions over extended periods of time, though interpreters often use more broad, complex movements. In addi-tion to the repetitive motions, professional interpreters often experience a high level of stress, splitting their attention in many ways, working in front of an "audience," frequently attending to the speaker, and simultaneously interacting with the student who is deaf or hard of hearing. Some report feeling strong somatic/emo-tional responses when interpreting something with which they strongly disagree, having to put on a facade of neutrality while maintaining a professional demeanor. Interpreters usually work at the speaker's pace and generally experience a lack of control in their work. Most report a desire for perfection because they have the responsibility to interpret as accurately as possible. Similarly, people working on computers with time pressures, such as news-paper employees, show very high rates of RMIs (Sauter, Hales, Bernard, Fine, Peterson, Putz-Anderson, Scheifer, & Ochs, 1993).

Purpose

The purpose of this research was to explore the psychophysio-logical correlates, within a systems perspective, associated with sign language interpreting and derive possible strategies to prevent discomfort and pain. Recent studies have suggested the develop-ment of a safe signing style that incorporates smooth, relaxed sign-ing; few hand-wrist deviations; and adequate rest breaks (DeCaro et al; 1992; Norris, 1996; Montgomery, 1996; Spaulding, 1996; National Technical Institute for the Deaf, Undated). This research goes beyond the signing and work style by investigating the physiologi-cal changes before, during, and after interpreting.

Methodology

Subjects
Nine (five pilot) volunteer subjects who were part-time or full-time professional sign language interpreters at SFSU.

Sensor Location and Equipment
Left and right surface electromyographic activity (sEMG) were recorded from the upper trapezius and forearm extensor/flexor muscles; respiration was recorded with a strain gauge 2 in. above the umbilicus; peripheral temperature was recorded from the left index finger; and skin conductance (EDG) was recorded from the ring and middle fingers of the left hand. Physiological signals were recorded with a Flexcomp (Thought Technology, Ltd.) and sampled at 32 times per second.

Procedure
After completing a history and symptom checklist, sensors were attached. The pre-baseline recording consisted of one minute each sitting and standing. Subjects then interpreted a 15-minute segment of a standardized audiotaped lecture to a video camera. This was videotaped to simulate a "real" work setting, since they were told that a deaf person would watch it. Post-baseline recording consisted of one minute each sitting and standing. At the end, subjects completed a post-assessment questionnaire.

Results

With commencement of interpreting, respiration rate increased (average 70%) and remained rapid, shallow, and thoracic throughout the task as is shown in Figure 1; respiration rate also increased when subjects expected to begin interpreting as shown in Figure 2. Average hand temperature was cold (73.9°F; SD 3.47°F) and decreased during interpreting (70.8°F; SD 2.38°F); while skin conductance increased (average 50%) and remained high during interpreting as is shown in Figure 3. Muscles were held slightly contracted (see Figure 4), even during pauses, indicating that no microbreaks were taken, thereby preventing regeneration. Most subjects were unaware of the significant changes in their bodies. They expressed surprise when their own records were reviewed.

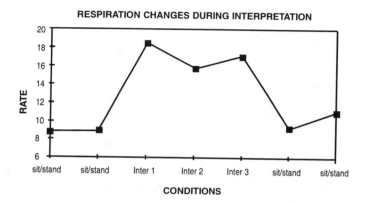

Figure 1. Average respiration rate during 15-minute interpreting session (n=4). Note the significant increase in breathing rate while interpreting (Inter 1, Inter 2, Inter 3).

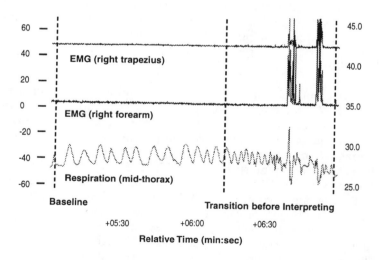

Figure 2. Individual respiration trace showing an increase in respiration rate when anticipating interpreting. The increased respiration rate continued during the 15 minutes of interpreting.

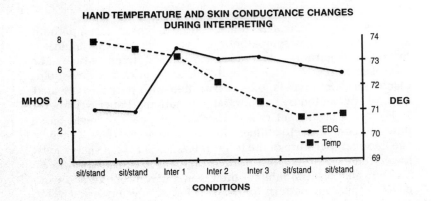

Figure 3. Average hand temperature and skin conductance during the 15-minute interpreting session (n=4). Note the initial cool hand temperature that continued to decrease with a concurrent initial increase in skin conductance, which remained elevated during interpreting (Inter 1, Inter 2, Inter 3).

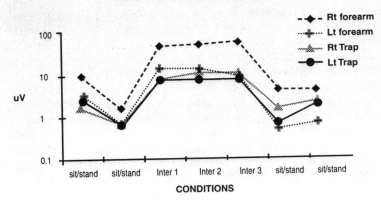

Figure 4. Average sEMG changes during 15-minute interpreting session (n=4). Note that all four muscle groups increased in muscle tension and remained tense during interpreting.

Discussion

These physiological responses suggest chronic sympathetic arousal. When high sympathetic arousal continues, as indicated by rapid breathing, decreased peripheral temperature, and increased skin conductance, individuals are at risk of developing discomfort. Cold hands, often associated with performance anxiety and augmented by shallow, rapid breathing (Peper & Tibbetts, 1994), are a significant risk factor. They indicate reduced blood flow and contribute to stiffness in the hands and wrists. The average hand temperature of the interpreters (73.9°F) was significantly lower than observed in a normal population[4] (86.9°F, SD 8.8°F). This chronic arousal inhibits the regenerative process, and exacerbates the pain pattern found with RMIs. The increased sEMG activity with few microbreaks suggests that muscle tissue is less likely to regenerate during interpreting and this may lead to the development of tender trigger points, especially if the interpreter is breathing rapidly and shallowly. If one has tender trigger points, a chronic state of high sympathetic arousal contributes to a deleterious cycle of pain (McNulty, Gevirtz, Hubbard, & Berkoff, 1994).

To reduce the risk of RMI, this physiological profile suggests that interpreters need to become aware of their physiological responses, both in anticipation of and during interpreting. They need to learn preventive work strategies such as breathing effortlessly, warming hands, and taking microbreaks. These interventions would lower sympathetic arousal and allow somatic regeneration. A similar approach was successfully used to reduce the incidence of RMI symptoms with individuals working at computers (Shumay & Peper, 1996). We expect that similar preventive interventions also would be successful for sign language interpreters. When interpreters integrate these skills into their work patterns, they may prevent or decrease discomfort. Thereby, Workers' Compensation claims may be significantly reduced, and interpreters may extend their professional careers, improve the quality of their lives, and rediscover the joy of interpreting.

References

DeCaro, J., Feuerstein, M., & Hurwitz, T. A. (1992). Cumulative trauma disorders among educational interpreters: Contributing factors and intervention. *American Annals of the Deaf, 137* (3), 288-292.

Mc Nulty, W. H., Gevirtz, R. N., Hubbard, D. R. & Berkoff, G. M. (1994). Needle electromyographic evaluation of trigger point response to a psychological stressor. *Psychophysiology, 31,* 313-216.

Montgomery, K. (1996). The body is not a robot!: Options for diagnosis and treatment of carpal tunnel syndrome. *The Registry of Interpreters for the Deaf (RID), VIEWS, 13* (1), 14-16.

National Technical Institute for the Deaf. (Undated). *Cumulative Trauma Disorders.* College of the Rochester Institute of Technology & U.S. Department of Education.

Norris, R. (1996). Repetitive strain injuries (RSI) in sign language interpreters: Evaluation, treatment and prevention. *The Registry of Interpreters for the Deaf (RID), VIEWS, 13* (1), 1,30-31.

Peper, E. & Tibbetts, V. (1994). Effortless diaphragmatic breathing. *Physical Therapy Products, 6* (2), 67-71.

Peper, E., Wilson, V. S., Taylor, W., Pierce, A., Bender, K., & Tibbetts, V. (1994). Repetitive strain injury. Prevent computer user injury with biofeedback: Assessment and training protocol. *Physical Therapy Products, 5* (5), 17-22.

Sauter, S., Hales, T., Bernard, B., Fine, L., Petersen, M., Putz-Anderson, V., Schleifer, L., & Ochs, T. (1993). Summary of two NIOSH field studies of musculoskeletal disorders and VDT work among telecommunications and newspaper workers. In Luczak, H., Cakir, A. and Cakir, G (Eds). *Work With Display Units* (p. 229-234). New York: Elsevier Science Publishers B.V.

Shumay, D. & Peper, E. (1996). Group training strategies for using biofeedback to prevent computer-related disorders. *Proceedings of the International Congress on Stress and Health,* (p. 52). Sidney, Australia: The University of Sydney

Spaulding, C. (1996). Prevention training: An inoculation against cumulative trauma disorders. *The Registry of Interpreters for the Deaf (RID), VIEWS, 13,* (1).

Footnotes

[1] We are deeply indebted to Tony Moy and the interpreters at the SFSU Disabilities Resource Center who provided time and commitment, and Marcia Allsopp from Human Resources. We thank Lynne Giere and Llew Keller for their significant contributions to the study. We also thank Vicci Tibbetts, Rick Harvey, Dianne Shumay, and Mark Armstrong for their assistance.

[2] Adapted from Gibney, K.H. and Peper, E. (1997). *Healthy Interpreting*. San Francisco State University.

[3] For more information, contact: Erik Peper, Ph.D., IHHS, San Francisco State University, 1600 Holloway Ave., San Francisco, CA 94132. e-mail: ihhs@sfsu.edu

[4] Average hand temperature recorded from 94 college students at SFSU.

Journal of Interpretation

Sign Language Interpreters: Simultaneous Interpreting and Memory

Christopher Haas, M.A., CI and CT

Sign Language Interpreters: Simultaneous Interpreting and Memory

Christopher Haas, M.A., CI and CT

Abstract

This research examines the relationship between the interpreting process and content retention. Sign language interpreters simultaneously interpret two narratives: one from spoken English to American Sign Language (ASL) and the other from ASL to spoken English. The interpreters are tested on their retention of the content of each narrative after completing the task. The interpreters' scores are compared to the scores of two control groups. The results show that the "listeners" have better overall retention of content than the interpreters, regardless of the direction of the interpretation. When the interpreters are divided according to language background, differences are found. Interpreters who grew up with sign language exposure may have an advantage over interpreters who learn sign language later in life. The results show that the interpreters who grew up with sign language score higher on overall retention than the interpreters who learn sign language as a second language.

Introduction

Sign language interpreting is a multi-task process. The interpreter must receive the source language, analyze it for meaning, determine an idiomatically equivalent target message, produce that target, and monitor that target as the input of a new source message starts the cycle all over. Often the interpreter is performing these tasks simultaneously. With the sheer volume and complexity of information that is handled during the interpreting process, one wonders how much of that information the interpreter is able to retain after the fact. Does the interpreting process impede the formation of memory? How accurately and how much of the message content can the interpreter remember after completing the task of simultaneously interpreting that content into another language?

Some understanding of human memory is necessary in

order to discuss the relationship between retention and the interpreting process. Current theory represents human memory as a process that occurs in stages. The first stage is the sensory register. All stimuli from the physical world enter the human mind through the five senses. At this stage, information is imprinted in the sensory register as a perfect and identical representation of the original stimulus. Unfortunately, this representation only lasts one to two seconds. Information that does not go on to the next stage of memory decays and is lost (Wingfield & Byrnes, 1981).

The second stage of human memory is short-term memory (STM). All conscious processes occur in STM. This stage acts as a filter for the infinite amount of information that enters the sensory register. STM is estimated to hold from five to nine chunks of information for approximately 18 seconds. Stimulus that is emotionally charged, interesting, or consciously attended to moves into STM. In this stage, one can rehearse the information by thinking about it or mentally repeating it. Through this conscious cognitive action, the stimulus is retained in STM. If the information is not rehearsed or attended to, it is forgotten (Wingfield & Byrnes, 1981).

With rehearsal or attention, information can enter the third stage of human memory known as long-term memory (LTM). LTM is thought to fall into two categories. The deliberate attempt to memorize information is called effortful memory. Information that is emotionally charged or significant to the individual seems to enter LTM automatically via a process called effortless memory. All knowledge and skill is contained in LTM. LTM is believed to be limitless in both capacity and duration (Wingfield & Byrnes, 1981).

Information is processed in STM and potentially stored in LTM. Stored information is retrieved from LTM and brought to conscious awareness in STM. The failure of information to enter LTM can be the result of competing processes in STM. If multiple stimuli are present in STM, the information not attended to will be lost (Wingfield & Byrnes, 1981).

The interpreter's task requires the use of both STM and LTM. There is an equilibrium of information flow that must be maintained by STM in which new information continuously enters and replaces the old. If processing time is too long or too much information is present in STM, then information will be lost (Cokely, 1992). This idea seems to describe the continuous turnover of stimuli experienced during the interpreting task. It suggests that there is little opportunity for rehearsal in STM and encoding in LTM. Robinson (1987) states that lag time in the interpreting process relies on STM capacity and that there is coordination with LTM to retrieve the meaning of stimuli as it enters STM.

If there are at least two processes occurring at the same time in STM during the interpreting task, can the interpreter attend to all of the information adequately enough for it to be encoded in LTM? It might seem that incoming source messages and outgoing target messages would compete for the interpreter's attention in STM. Some information may be of particular interest to the interpreter and effortlessly encoded in LTM. In theory, the interpreter would have to make some kind of effort to encode any neutral information in LTM.

Literature Review

There are three standard measures of information retention: recall, recognition, and relearning. Recall requires the retrieval of specific items from LTM. "Fill-in-the-blank" tests, in which one must retrieve the correct data on demand, are commonly used to assess recall (Bolles, 1988; Wingfield & Byrnes, 1981). Recognition is usually based on a sense of familiarity with an item. Multiple-choice tests, in which one must choose the correct item from a group of potential answers, are often used to assess recognition. A third measure of memory is the phenomenon of relearning. To test this, the time it takes for a subject to learn new information is recorded. When it appears that the material is forgotten, the subject relearns the information and the time is again recorded. The fact that subjects typically relearn the information in a shorter period of time is attributed to memory (Wingfield & Byrnes, 1981).

It is unclear what, if any, relationship exists between recall and recognition. It has been proposed that recall and recognition are different stages of the same process. Recognition is often considered to be the easier task. It is one thing to know a face in the crowd (recognition) and another thing to put a name to that face (recall). Overall, memory is better if the stimuli are organized and have meaning. The basis of human memory is order and meaning. Random, nonsensical stimuli are not conducive to either recall or recognition. Recall is thought to be more order-dependent since one may have to go through a chronological series of memories before arriving at the desired piece of information. Recognition is thought to be more context-dependent in the sense that retrieval is more successful if associated stimuli are also present (Bolles, 1988). It is sometimes harder to recognize a co-worker encountered in a non-work environment.

It has also been proposed that recall and recognition are separate processes. However, recall is still considered to be the harder task and one that requires more effort. Recognition is viewed as automatic retrieval that is triggered by associated stimuli (Wingfield & Byrnes, 1981). Being an automatic process, recognition would be faster and more accurate than recall (Arnold, 1984).

Some research on the interpreting process of spoken languages and memory has been done. There are opposing theories on the accuracy and amount of source information that the interpreter retains in LTM after completing the interpreting task. The goal of much of the research has been to establish if the interpreting process, by its very nature, interferes with the formation of LTM or reinforces it (Ingram, 1992).

After the interpretation of a cohesive discourse, recall may be fairly good because strong coherence implies sense and meaning, which aid LTM. However, it is possible that the incoming source message interferes with the encoding of the preceding message in LTM (Robinson, 1987). There is some speculation that language interpreters retain very little of the content that they interpret. Mahmoodzadel (1992) proposes that it is almost impossible for the interpreter to remember the message content because the interpreting process occupies too much of the interpreter's STM capacity to allow for proper encoding in LTM. Daro (1989) states that the interpreter is not motivated to remember the message and that the interpreter's attention is so divided during the task that the information is not stored in LTM.

Another theory suggests that bilingual persons may have better retention than monolingual persons (LeNy, 1978). Because of the nature of their work, all interpreters are bilingual. The suggestion is that bilinguals have two separate memory systems; one for each language (O'Neil, Roy & Tremblay, 1993; Paivio & Begg, 1981). In theory, when the bilingual interprets from one language to another, both memory systems are activated and have a commonality on the semantic level. Recall by a bilingual person, with two memory systems, would be better than recall by a monolingual person, in which only one memory system can be activated. It is believed that the utilization of two memory systems makes for stronger memory and increases the likelihood of retrieval (Paivio & Begg, 1981).

Typically, research on the interpreting task and memory is based on a comparison of listening versus interpreting. That is, a subject's retention is tested after a single task (listening to information), and a subject's retention is tested after a dual task (interpreting information). Others have compared retention after shadowing tasks with retention after interpreting tasks. The results of studies can seem contradictory. Daro (1989) finds no significant difference in subjects' ability to retain information in LTM after either interpreting tasks or shadowing tasks. It has been suggested that the depth of processing involved in a task is directly related to retention. A study found that recognition after listening or reading is better than recognition after interpreting or sight translating. The rationale is that one could devote full attention and processing capacity to the single task of listening or reading. The dual task of interpreting or sight translating divides one's attention and processing capacity, which is not conducive to retention (Viezzi, 1990). On the other hand, it is suggested that the recall and recognition of interpreted information is greater than the recall and recognition of shadowed information (ONeil, Roy & Tremblay, 1993).

Lambert (1989) studied the recognition and recall of interpreted information immediately following a task. Listening, as a single task, was used as the control condition. The listener can devote full attention and processing capacity to the task. Simultaneous interpreting is a complex task in which one must analyze both message input and output. Surprisingly, recall after listening and simultaneous interpreting was found to be equivalent. Recognition after listening was significantly better than recognition after simultaneous interpreting. It would seem that the dual task of simultaneous interpreting interferes on some level with the depth of processing that is possible (Lambert, 1989).

There is a limited amount of research that focuses on sign language interpreting (versus spoken language interpreting) and memory. Ingram (1987) found that content recognition improved after interpreting or transliterating sign language. These tasks involve a deeper level of processing, which leads to stronger retention. Later, Ingram (1992) compared retention after listening tasks, interpreting tasks, and shadowing tasks. Recall after the single task of listening was best. Recall after the interpreting task was better than recall after the shadowing task. The recognition of meaning was better than the recognition of form regardless of the task involved. Overall, the recognition of meaning after interpreting and transliterating sign language tasks was better than recognition of meaning after the listening task. The results suggest that the two languages use separate memory capacities and that two memory capacities reinforce one another to produce better retention of content (Ingram, 1992). Isham and Lane (1993) suggest that the act of sign language interpreting immediately involves LTM during semantic processing. They found that recall is equal for listening tasks and interpreting tasks because both occur at the semantic level.

Research Questions

The original question remains: What relationship is there between the interpreting process and post-task memory? The field of sign language interpreting is bi-directional by its very nature. The published research on sign language interpreting and content retention does not address the potential differences that may exist because of this situation. Lambert (1989) comments that spoken language interpreters typically work from their second language ("B" language) to their native language ("A" language). This is one of the most striking differences between sign language and spoken language interpreting. Sign language interpreters are required to work both from their "B" language into their "A" language and from their "A" language into their "B" language. Seleskovitch (1978) concurs that the simultaneous interpreter usually cannot successfully work into the "B" language; he/she generally does not perform as well when working into the second language. Simultaneous interpreting can only be done properly into one's native language unless one is a true bilingual (Seleskovitch, 1978). The current study will address the issue of content retention after the interpreting process versus retention after a "listening" task. This study will also deal with the issue of content retention and the interpreting process in terms of the direction of the interpretation.

Methodology

Two videotapes were recorded for this research, one in ASL and the other in spoken English. A female, native signer provided the ASL narrative and described a series of anecdotes from her childhood. A female, native speaker of English provided the spoken English narrative and told a child's story. Both videotape segments were approximately 13 minutes in length. An 18-question test was created based on the content of each narrative. Each test consisted of a balanced mix of "fill in the blank" and multiple-choice questions. The "fill in the blank" type questions required the recall of specific information and the multiple-choice type questions required the recognition of familiar information, (Bolles, 1988). The tests were graded to determine the percentage of correct recall and recognition of semantic information from the narratives.

The interpreters were asked to simultaneously interpret the narrative and take the respective test for that narrative immediately upon completion of the task. Then the same format was followed for the second narrative. Each interpreter was provided with an "audience": a Deaf person for the spoken English to ASL condition and a hearing person for the ASL to spoken English condition. One interpreter did not have a Deaf "audience" for the spoken English to ASL condition, but that interpreter's scores seem to be compatible with the other participants in the study.

Two control groups of "listeners" were included for comparison purposes. Three Deaf listeners watched the ASL narrative and took the same test as the interpreters did. Three hearing listeners watched the spoken English narrative and took the same test as the interpreters. All participants were told of the nature of the study and given the same background information. The interpreters' scores were compared to the control group scores for the respective conditions. The interpreters' scores were also compared within group for the respective tasks.

Subjects

Nine interpreters participated in the study. All of the interpreters held either the RID Comprehensive Skills Certificate (CSC), the Certificate of Interpreting (CI), or both. Four of the interpreters stated that their first language is ASL/sign language and spoken English. One interpreter listed Spanish and English as first languages. The four remaining interpreters identified spoken English as their first language. There were five females and four males. The interpreters in the study indicated that they had studied sign language for a range of 5 to 25 years. Two stated that they had studied it all their lives. The participants had been interpreting for a range of 5 to 20 years. One stated that he/she had interpreted all his/her life.

The three Deaf "listeners" in the control group were all female and fluent signers. The three hearing "listeners" in the control group included two females and one male. All of the "listeners" were asked to watch only the respective narrative for their group (a single task).

Results

The interpreters' scores were compared to the appropriate control group scores depending on the direction of the interpretation. The nine interpreters simultaneously interpreted the ASL narrative to spoken English and received a total mean score of 80% content retention. The Deaf control group's total mean score was 84% retention for the ASL narrative. These scores can be sub-divided for recall and recognition. The total mean score for recall was 78% by the interpreters and 80% by the Deaf control group. The total mean score for recognition was 83% by the interpreters and 89% by the Deaf control group. The "listeners" did better on all measures than the interpreters. Both groups did better with recognition than recall, as theory would predict (see Tables 1 and 2).

Table 1
Deaf "Listeners": ASL Narrative

	Recall	Recognition	Total Retention
Listener #1	61%	78%	69%
Listener #2	78%	100%	89%
Listener #3	100%	89%	94%
Group Mean	**80%**	**89%**	**84%**

Table 2
Simultaneous Interpreting: ASL to Spoken English

	Recall	Recognition	Total Retention
Interpreter #1	56%	78%	67%
Interpreter #2	89%	89%	89%
Interpreter #3	78%	78%	78%
Interpreter #4	89%	78%	83%
Interpreter #5	89%	89%	89%
Interpreter #6	56%	78%	67%
Interpreter #7	78%	78%	78%
Interpreter #8	100%	89%	94%
Interpreter #9	67%	89%	78%
Group Mean	**78%**	**83%**	**80%**

Tables 3 and 4 provide summary data on how the interpreters and "hearing listeners" compared in dealing with spoken English. The nine interpreters simultaneously interpreted the spoken English narrative to ASL and received a total mean score of 71% content retention. By comparison, the hearing control group's total mean score was 82% for the spoken English narrative. The total mean score for recall was 68% by the interpreters and 83% by the hearing control group. The total mean score for recognition was 74% by the interpreters and 80% by the hearing control group. Again, the "listeners" did better on all measures than the interpreters. The interpreters did better with recognition than recall, and the "listeners" did better with recall than recognition.

Table 3
Simultaneous Interpreting: Spoken English to ASL

	Recall	Recognition	Total Retention
Interpreter #1	33%	72%	53%
Interpreter #2	67%	100%	83%
Interpreter #3	94%	67%	81%
Interpreter #4	72%	67%	69%
Interpreter #5	72%	67%	69%
Interpreter #6	67%	78%	72%
Interpreter #7	61%	89%	75%
Interpreter #8	72%	78%	75%
Interpreter #9	78%	44%	61%
Group Mean	**68%**	**74%**	**71%**

Table 4
Hearing "Listeners": Spoken English Narrative

	Recall	Recognition	Total Retention
Listener #1	78%	94%	86%
Listener #2	94%	67%	81%
Listener #3	78%	78%	78%
Group Mean	**83%**	**80%**	**82%**

Based on the background information gathered for this research, the interpreters can be divided into two groups and their scores can be compared. Four interpreters noted that they had been exposed to ASL or some sign language all of their lives. Five interpreters can be more formally described as second-language learners of ASL.

The four interpreters who grew up with ASL or sign language had a total mean score of 88% content retention when working from ASL to spoken English. Their total mean score for recall was 89% and the total mean score for recognition was 86% for this condition (see Table 5). When working from ASL to spoken English, the five interpreters who learned ASL as a second language had a total mean score of 75% content retention. For this condition, their total mean score for recall was 69% and the total mean score for recognition was 80% (see Table 6).

Table 5
Simultaneous Interpreting: ASL to Spoken English
Grew up with ASL or Sign Language

	Recall	Recognition	Total Retention
Interpreter #2	89%	89%	89%
Interpreter #3	78%	78%	78%
Interpreter #5	89%	89%	89%
Interpreter #8	100%	89%	94%
Group Mean	**89%**	**86%**	**88%**

Table 6
Simultaneous Interpreting: ASL to Spoken English
Learned ASL as a Second Language

	Recall	Recognition	Total Retention
Interpreter #1	56%	78%	67%
Interpreter #4	89%	78%	83%
Interpreter #6	56%	78%	67%
Interpreter #7	78%	78%	78%
Interpreter #9	67%	89%	78%
Group Mean	**69%**	**80%**	**75%**

The four interpreters who grew up with exposure to ASL or sign language had a total mean score of 77% content retention when working from spoken English to ASL. Their total mean score for recall was 76%, and the total mean score for recognition was 78% for this condition (see Table 7). When working from spoken English to ASL, the five interpreters who learned ASL as a second language had a total mean score of 66%. Their total mean score for recall was 62%, and the total mean score for recognition was 70% for this condition (see Table 8).

Table 7
Simultaneous Interpreting: Spoken English to ASL
Grew up with ASL or Sign Language

	Recall	Recognition	Total Retention
Interpreter #2	67%	100%	83%
Interpreter #3	94%	67%	81%
Interpreter #5	72%	67%	69%
Interpreter #8	72%	78%	75%
Group Mean	**76%**	**78%**	**77%**

Table 8
Simultaneous Interpreting: Spoken English to ASL
Learned ASL as a Second Language

	Recall	Recognition	Total Retention
Interpreter #1	33%	72%	53%
Interpreter #4	72%	67%	69%
Interpreter #6	67%	78%	72%
Interpreter #7	61%	89%	75%
Interpreter #9	78%	44%	61%
Group Mean	**62%**	**70%**	**66%**

Discussion

As a group, the nine interpreters had better retention when working from ASL into spoken English than when working from spoken English into ASL (80% versus 71%, respectively). For both conditions, the control groups received higher scores than the interpreters as a group for both recall and recognition. These results might suggest that the complex task of interpreting, regardless of the direction, created more interference to content retention than the single task of listening. However, that tendency is not quite so clear when the nine interpreters are divided according to language background.

Theory states that interpreters will perform better when working into their native language (Seleskovitch, 1978). One might expect the five interpreters who learned ASL as a second language to score higher on content retention when working from ASL (B language) into spoken English (A language). The results support this assumption (75% versus 66% when working from spoken English into ASL). These five interpreters scored higher on recognition than recall regardless of the direction of their interpretation. This result would fit the assumption that recognition is an easier task than recall. Both control groups did better than the five interpreters on all measures of retention. Hearing "listeners" had a total mean score of 82%, and Deaf "listeners" had a total mean score of 84%.

The four interpreters who grew up with exposure to ASL or sign language also scored higher on content retention when working from ASL into spoken English (88% versus 77% when working from spoken English into ASL). These four interpreters scored slightly better on recognition than recall when working from spoken English to ASL. They scored slightly better on recall than recognition when working from ASL into spoken English. Hearing "listeners" scored higher on all measures of retention than these four interpreters when working from spoken English into ASL (82% versus 77%, respectively). When working from ASL into spoken English, the four interpreters scored higher overall than Deaf "listeners" (88% versus 84%, respectively).

The study made use of videotaped narratives to ensure consistency of the source messages. Some of the interpreters who participated commented that in a live situation they might have asked for repetition of information or asked the speakers to slow down. All of the participants agreed that the videotape quality for both narratives was clear and satisfactory. No evaluation of the quality of the interpretations was included in the scope of this study. Additionally, there was no determination if failure to retain information by any of the subjects was due to actual forgetting or a lack of source comprehension. All memory tests were administered in written English. It is unknown what impact other modalities of presentation might have produced. All tests were administered immediately upon completion of the task. It is unknown if retention scores would have been consistent over time. The source narratives were assumed to be equitable enough for comparison, and the respective tests were assumed to be of equal difficulty.

Conclusion

The results suggest that the process of simultaneous sign

language interpreting may interfere with the retention of content. This interference may be more prominent when the interpreter is working from spoken English into ASL. As a group, the interpreters had better retention of content when working from ASL into spoken English. Those interpreters who grew up with exposure to ASL or sign language appear to have an advantage over interpreters who learn ASL as a second language. Interpreters who grew up with ASL or sign language scored higher on all measures of retention than interpreters who learned ASL as a second language, regardless of the direction of the interpretation.

References

Arnold, M. B. (1984). *Memory and the brain*. New Jersey: Lawrence Erlbaum Associates, Publishers.

Bolles, E. B. (1988). *Remembering and forgetting*. New York: Walker and Co.

Cokely, D. R. (1992). *Interpretation: a sociolinguistic model*. Maryland: Linstok Press.

Daro, V. (1989). The role of memory and attention in simultaneous interpretation: a neurolinguistic approach. *The Interpreter's Newsletter (2)*.

Ingram, R. M. (1987). Simultaneous interpretation of sign languages: semiotic and psycholinguistic perspectives. *1987 educators pedagogical institute readings on interpretation* (pp. 91102). Amsterdam: Mouton Publishers.

Ingram, R. M. (1992). Interpreters' recognition of structure & meaning. In D. Cokely (Ed.), Sign language interpreters and interpreting, (pp. 99119). Maryland: Linstok Press.

Isham, W.P. & Lane, H. (1993). Simultaneous interpretation and the recall of sourcelanguage sentences. *Language and cognitive processes, 8, 241264*. Massachusetts: VSP Publications.

Lambert, S. (1989). Information processing among conference interpreters: a test of the depth of processing hypothesis. In Gran and Dodds (Eds.), Aspects of applied and experimental resear*ch on conference interpretation* (pp. 8391). Udine, Italy: Campanotto Editore.

LeNy. (1978). Psychosemantics and simultaneous interpretation. In Long & HardingEsch (Eds.), Summary and recall of text, (pp. 311312). New York: Harper Press.

Mahmoodzadel, K. (1992). Consecutive interpreting: Its principles and techniques. In Dollerup & Loddengaard (Eds.), *Teaching translation and interpreting* (pp. 231236). Pennsylvania: J. Benjamins Publishing Co.

O'Neil, W., Roy, L. and Tremblay, R. (1993). A translation based generation effect in bilingual recall and recognition. *Memory and cognition, 21,* 488495.

Paivio, A. and Begg, I. (1981). Psychology of language. New Jersey: PrenticeHall.

Robinson, R. (1987). Visual memory and lag time. In 1987 RID convention. Maryland: RID Publications.

Seleskovitch, D. (1978). Interpreting for international conferences. Washington DC: Pen and Booth.

Viezzi, M. (1990). Sight translation, simultaneous interpretation
     and information retention. In Gran and Taylor (Eds.),
     *Aspects of applied and experimental research on conference
     interpretation* (pp. 5460). Udine, Italy: Campanotto Editore.
Wingfield, A. & Byrnes, D. L. (1981). The psychology of human
     memory. New York: Academic Press.

Journal of Interpretation

Saving Face: The Interpreter and Politeness

Jack Hoza, CSC, CI and CT
University of New Hampshire at Manchester

An ASL version of this paper is available on videotape (signed in ASL by the author). Those interested should send 1) a blank VHS videotape cassette and 2) a large self-addressed stamped envelope (in which to return the videotape) to: Jack Hoza, Director, Sign Language Interpretation, UNH-Manchester, 400 Commercial Street, Manchester, NH 03102. (Note: Requests can only be honored during the academic year—Sept. 1 through May 15.)

Saving Face: The Interpreter and Politeness

Jack Hoza, CSC, CI and CT
University of New Hampshire at Manchester

Abstract

Face — the positive social value a person claims for oneself or one's group — is an integral part of human interaction. Interlocutors have their own face needs and use politeness strategies to save the face of others. Mismatches in politeness strategies may 1) result in negative impressions, 2) have implications in power dynamics, and 3) cause a person to feel ashamed, inferior, confused, or flustered, i.e., to lose face. This paper uses an interactional sociolinguistic framework to explore the interpreter's impact on the face needs of the speakers in interpreted interaction. To explore this question, the paper makes use of real-life scenarios in which interpreters have unwittingly made decisions regarding face. First, the scenarios are analyzed using current interpreter metaphors and models of interpretation. Next, face and politeness systems are introduced, and the implications of mismatches in politeness strategies are discussed. Finally, the scenarios are revisited in light of this interactional sociolinguistic framework, and this framework is used to address the following question: How does the interpreter mediate speakers' face needs and politeness strategies?

1. Introduction

Interpreting for people who use different languages and have different cultural backgrounds is an intriguing and challenging process. While interpreters have seen major changes in how the field of American Sign Language-English (ASL-English) interpretation conceptualizes the interpreting process and the interpreter's role, current models of interpretation do not always provide interpreters with the guidance they need as they encounter and make decisions about scenarios such as the following, taken from an actual interpreting situation.[1]

Situation #1

The only new Deaf hire of some 200 new employees is taking a week-long training at the new job site. During his breaks on the first day, he relates to the interpreters that he has been frustrated with the difficulty the referral service is having in finding interpreters to cover the whole week and that he is disappointed in the lack of advancement opportunities at this job. On the second day, one of his immediate supervisors asks him how things are going. Without blinking an eye, he responds that he is very frustrated because of the lack of interpreters and the limited potential for advancement. The interpreter hesitates a second, then voices the comment by softening it a bit in the English rendition by first saying, "Things are going pretty well, but there are two things I really need to talk to you about."

The issue presented in this situation goes beyond the scope of current conceptualizations of interpretation. Current interpreter metaphors and models provide general guidance in decisions related to language and culture; however, in this case, the interpreter is attempting to mediate more than a linguistic or cultural difference. What is actually at stake here? In the interpreter's mind, the *relationship* between the new employee and the supervisor is foregrounded, and she makes the decision that a literal interpretation would adversely affect that relationship and how the new Deaf employee is seen. Current models and metaphors do not offer specific guidance for interpreters in such situations, but the interpreter here opts to mediate the relationship by adding a comment that was not stated by the Deaf employee.

Let us look at another real-life scenario:

Situation #2

The interpreter is having some difficulty interpreting for a hearing person and a Deaf person who work together because the topic under discussion is not very familiar to the interpreter (i.e., the speakers have a lot of shared background knowledge), so the interpreter pauses occasionally to process the information (and to seek clarification at times) in order to convey it accurately in the alternate language. At one point, the interpreter is voicing for the Deaf person and is taking such a processing pause when the Deaf person looks patiently at the interpreter and pauses for the interpreter to catch up. The hearing person interprets the pause (by both the interpreter and the Deaf person) as a signal to jump in and does so. The interpreter says in a polite manner, "Excuse me a second. The interpreter was just catching up," and proceeds to render an interpretation of the Deaf person's comments.

In this scenario, the awkward situation is the result of the interpreting process and its effect on the *interaction* of the parties. If the interpreter does nothing to correct the situation, the Deaf person may feel interrupted or the hearing person may feel embarrassed for having interrupted. It is important to note that the hearing and Deaf participants are trying to be cooperative and are trying to manage the interpreted interaction given the turn-taking regulators as they each perceive them. The interpreter, on the other hand, is struggling with the interpreting process and handling the interaction. There is more to this situation than the hearing person merely interrupting the Deaf person. Again, interpreters need more specific guidelines in dealing with such situations. Let's look at a third real-life scenario:

Situation #3

The interpreter is interpreting a graduate course in education, and the class — made up of many hearing students and only one Deaf student — has broken up into small groups, and students are taking turns providing each other feedback on educational posters they designed for special needs children. The hearing students are saying things like, "I especially like the pictures you chose because they are really eye-catching, and the concept you are expressing is clear, but I'm wondering if you thought about the lettering. Cursive may be a bit difficult for these students to read."

When the Deaf student provides feedback, she says (in ASL), "Actually, the color of the poster seems a bit dull. You should make use of a brighter color. These students may not even notice the poster unless it really catches their eye, but I agree that the pictures are really clear and the poster focuses on only one concept, which is nice for this group of students."

The interpreter thinks for a moment, then voices (by expressing the information in a different order), "I agree that the poster focuses on only one concept which is nice for this group of students and the pictures are really clear, but I'm wondering about the color because it may not catch the children's eye. Perhaps a brighter color would work better for that."

In this third scenario, the interpreter reverses the order of the information presented by the Deaf student. That is, the Deaf student is providing negative critique/feedback first, then positive feedback, but the interpreter presents the comments as positive feedback first, then negative critique/feedback second. The Deaf student states her feedback rather directly in her first sentence, ("Actually, the color of the poster seems a bit dull") and in the sentence that follows, she uses the modal *should* when she suggests making a change to the poster ("You should make use of a brighter color"). The interpreter, however, reframes the suggestion by using indirect strategies. First, she states the point of agreement or commonality, then she voices the negative feedback by using indirect phraseology: *I'm wondering* at the end of the first sentence ("I'm wondering about the color") and the words *perhaps* and *would* (instead of *should*) in the last sentence ("Perhaps a brighter color would work better for that").

What are the implications of this decision to reframe the feedback? Certainly, it has an effect on others' social perceptions of this individual. We can assume that the interpreter decides that the Deaf student's approach—if interpreted literally—would make her appear rather crude by seeming too direct, and that was clearly not the Deaf student's intent. In the interpreter's judgment, she is interpreting not only the speaker's goal of providing feedback in this situation, but she is also mediating how this feedback—and this person—is perceived by the Target Language group. In her view, the hearing students are using an explicit rule of politeness: say something nice first, then provide criticism couched in this positive comment. The interpreter is essentially *saving face* for the Deaf student by presenting the Deaf student as a polite, contributing member of the group, which is in keeping with the Deaf student's perceptions of the interaction.

In this paper, I propose that we use the contributions of politeness systems in the field of interactional sociolinguistics to provide elaboration on these issues. I argue that only by using this approach can we 1) account for the discourse differences in these scenarios, 2) make headway in understanding differences in politeness systems, and 3) provide interpreters with guidance in reaching the most appropriate decision in such situations.

Section 2 briefly reviews the metaphors and interpreting models that provide interpreters with different conceptions, or working models, of interpretation, and how each would interpret the situations given above. This section also highlights current trends in sociolinguistic research and the contributions of this paper. Section 3 briefly introduces the notions of face and politeness systems, and revisits the scenarios given above to clarify the interpreter's decision in each. Section 4 discusses the benefits of looking at these interpreter decisions in light of this interactional sociolinguistic approach and suggests possible areas for future research.

2. Interpreter Metaphors and Models

The metaphors and interpreting process models that interpreters have used to guide their work have changed over time. They have affected how interpreters think about their work and, therefore, have affected interpreters' judgment in particular situations. This section briefly reviews these metaphors and interpreting process models, and looks at how each resulting conceptualization would affect the interpreter's decisions in Situations 1-3 given above.

Metaphors
In this section, we first review the metaphors[2] that the field uses to discuss its work. Each metaphor provides a different framework for the interpreter's role and the interpreting process. The goal here is to highlight each framework and to

see their relative impact on how the three situations above would be defined and approached.

The machine and communication facilitator metaphors

The field of ASL-English interpretation has referred to the metaphor used in the early years of the profession as the *machine* metaphor, or *conduit* metaphor (Baker-Shenk, 1986; Witter-Merithew, 1986; Frishberg, 1990; Roy, 1993; Humphrey and Alcorn, 1995)[3]. Briefly, the focus of this metaphor is on interpreting the *language* of the participants,[4] with the assumption that the primary difference between Deaf people and hearing people can be explained by differences in language and modality (signed vs. spoken language). The assumption is that the responsibility of the interpreter is to convey each person's *words,* which would otherwise be inaccessible due to the modality difference. This model was modified as a later metaphor, *communication facilitator*, which expanded the linguistic view of interpretation as linguistic research on American Sign Language became more available[5]. The interpreter using this metaphor takes responsibility for using professional judgment related to the physical set-up of the interpreting environment and uses theory from the field of communication studies (e.g., sender/receiver models involving encoding and decoding) to aid in decisions related to relaying language. The focus of these metaphors is presented in Figure 1 below.

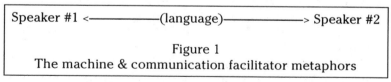

Speaker #1 <————————(language)————————> Speaker #2

Figure 1
The machine & communication facilitator metaphors

How the machine and communication facilitator metaphors address the situations given above is limited to the interpretation of *language* (albeit, the two metaphors would differ to some degree). In the first situation between the hearing supervisor and new Deaf employee, the interpreter's assumption would be to interpret the words of the Deaf employee so that the hearing supervisor would know what this person meant linguistically. In linguistics, this is referred to as "sentence meaning, language meaning devoid of context." The result would be a rather literal interpretation, something like: "I'm really frustrated with the fact that the referral service can't find interpreters for the whole week, and I really don't think this job is going to offer me any chance of promotion." This interpretation would not consider the wider social context of the utterance, which the interpreter in the actual scenario certainly did.

In the second situation, in which the hearing person interrupts, the interpreter would feel that s/he should not act on the interruption because the interpreter's role, as defined by these metaphors, is to stay out of the interaction and to only interpret people's *words*. So, although this interpreter may feel the situation is uncomfortable, s/he would see the responsibility of making any repairs as lying in the hands of the interlocutors, not the interpreter. The belief is that if the interpreter does anything other than interpret the language, consumers react with confusion, frustration, or distrust (Ford, 1981). In other words, the interpreter would most likely keep interpreting as though nothing had happened. The *interaction* of the participants would certainly not be a consideration in the interpreting process.

In the third situation, involving a Deaf student's feedback in a graduate course, an interpreter working under one of these metaphors would most likely interpret the Deaf student's comments as critique/feedback first, positive statement second, as it was produced in the Source Language by this student. In this case, as well as in the other two scenarios, implications of *face*, or *politeness*, would be beyond the scope of these metaphors and would most likely not be a consideration.

The cultural mediator metaphor

The *cultural mediator* metaphor, or *bilingual/bicultural* metaphor, expands the understanding of the interpreting task to include not only language, but also *culture*. The field has come to recognize that language and culture are inseparable, i.e., that language devoid of cultural content conveys limited meaning. This metaphor is shown graphically in Figure 2 below.

Speaker #1 <————(language/culture)————> Speaker #2

Figure 2
The cultural mediator or bilingual/bicultural metaphor

Now let us review how the *cultural mediator* metaphor would frame these three scenarios in terms of *language* and *culture*. In the first situation (between the hearing supervisor and new Deaf employee), the interpreter would consider the social context of the utterance and focus not only on sentence meaning, but would also consider speaker meaning, i.e., the speaker's goal in this situation and how that would be expressed in the Target Language. The interpreter, then, would realize a literal interpretation is not warranted, as the new employee intends only to express his frustration and to possibly seek support, but not to infuriate his new boss. So the real question is, How is this done in English? This metaphor considers the wider social/cultural context of the utterance in terms of speaker meaning and, while the exact nature of the cultural issue would be unclear to the interpreter, s/he would consider this a cultural adjustment and perhaps render an interpretation similar to what was given in this scenario.

In the second situation (in which the hearing person interrupts), the interpreter may well recognize that there was a cultural difference in turn-taking strategies and may be prompted to make a repair, as happens here. It is important to remember that the *process* of making this decision is based on linguistic and cultural norms (in this case, differing turn-taking regulators), which are assumed to be part of the interpreter's working model of interpretation.

In the third situation (the Deaf student's feedback in a graduate course), the interpreter may or may not make an adjustment in the order of the feedback items, i.e., the interpreter may interpret the comment as either critique/feedback first, positive statement second, or positive statement first, critique/feedback second. This decision would depend on the interpreter's knowledge and awareness of this rather vague notion of culture. The interpreter may or may not be aware of this specific cultural difference in order to mediate it.

The ally metaphor

A more recent metaphor, *ally*, has been explored to better understand the relationship between hearing interpreters and Deaf persons, and the power dynamics of the interpreted event (Baker-Shenk, 1992). The recognition of power relations and historical oppression were originally the impetus for this metaphor, but the metaphor has grown to more globally explore the relationships between interpreters and Deaf people, and how the interpreter can work with Deaf persons to equalize the communication access within interpreting settings (see Figure 3 below).

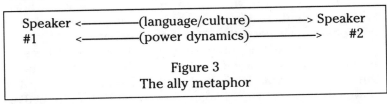

Figure 3
The ally metaphor

The ally metaphor would frame these situations not only in terms of language and culture, but also in terms of the power dynamics between, or among, the interlocutors. In the first situation (between the hearing supervisor and new Deaf employee), in addition to considering the linguistic meaning and the social context of the utterance, the interpreter would be mindful of the power relations. That is, the interpreter would recognize the Deaf person's effectiveness to *act* and communicate as intended in this situation, and to not feel disempowered because he is communicating through an interpreter. The interpreter, then, may choose to adjust the interpretation accordingly, resulting in a decision similar to what was done here, but for the purpose of not wanting to adversely affect the power dynamics.

Likewise, in the second situation (in which the hearing person interrupts), the *process* of making this decision would again be based on language, cultural norms, and power relations. The interpreter would most likely act to ensure that the Deaf person maintains the floor to maintain power. The interpreter's focus is on a sense of fairness in terms of power relations and, thus, the interpreter would look at his/her impact on changes in the power dynamics.

In the third situation (the Deaf student's feedback in a graduate course), the interpreter would feel a need to adjust the interpretation so that not only would the Deaf person's intent get across, but so that she would not feel looked down upon or be embarrassed because she is certainly not intending to communicate crassness. When the situation is framed in terms of the power dynamics, the interpreter considers whether or not the Deaf person would have less power if the interpreter conveys the message in a literal way. Again, the power dynamics of the situation would be a primary consideration.

An interactional mediator metaphor

This paper seeks to expand upon previous metaphors. While it assumes both the cultural mediator and ally metaphors, it suggests that the interpreter become aware that s/he is also mediating the *relationship* of the interlocutors by acting as an *interactional mediator*. The ally metaphor takes the first step in addressing this relationship by identifying power dynamics. I would argue that there is more to mediating a relationship than the vague notion of power dynamics; specifically face needs and politeness systems are involved (see Figure 4 below). In addition, there are likely other aspects to this interactional mediator metaphor yet to be explored. The "Current trends" section discusses this further.

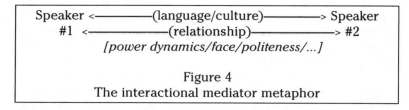

Figure 4
The interactional mediator metaphor

Summary

The difference in the metaphor used has a great impact on how the interpreter frames the nature of the interaction. When the helper or communication facilitator metaphor is used, the focus is exclusively on language. The resulting interpreter decisions fail to consider the wider context and, therefore, do not consider the social context or our topic here: saving face and politeness. When the cultural mediator metaphor or ally metaphor is used, we see that the interpreter is making decisions regarding the face of the speaker. However, the framework provided by each metaphor does not frame the situation in these terms. The interpreter may well sense that something is wrong and may feel a need to do something due to a vague notion like culture or power relations, but these metaphors only provide guidance on a general, or superficial, level. To more fully understand what these metaphors offer the field, it is necessary to further break them down, which is our goal here. Suggesting an interactional mediator metaphor offers another way of framing the interpreted event which, using research from interactional sociolinguistics and perhaps other fields, can provide further elaboration on the role and interpreting decisions of the interpreter.

Later, section 3 will elaborate on the notions of face and politeness systems, and provides interpreters with clearer guidance in situations such as the three discussed in this paper. However, first we will briefly review interpreting process models and current research trends on interpreted interaction to see what this research offers the field.

Interpreting process models and current trends

In this section, we discuss interpreting process models, recent research on interpreted interaction, and the implications of each on the expectations the interpreter brings to an interpreted event. Specifically, this section will show that current interpreting process models are limited in how they frame the interpreted interaction, and current research trends, including this paper, are elaborating the impact the interpreter has on the interaction.

Interpreting process models

Interpreting process models to date have focused on the process of going from the Source Language (SL) text to the Target Language (TL) text. These models have changed over the years. The earlier models were based largely on communication models (e.g., Ford, 1981; Ingram, 1985) and the current models (primarily psycholinguistic and sociolinguistic in nature) focus mostly on language, culture, and contextual meaning (namely, Cokely, 1992; Colonomos, 1992). The key components of current models are usually the following: analysis, understanding (mental representation), conveying equivalency, and monitoring the process[6]. While this is a simplification, it serves our purposes. Basically, these models are saying that the interpreter is a *message processor* whose responsibility it is to express the SL meaning expressed by Speaker #1 in the TL so that it is understood by Speaker #2. These models have enlightened the field; however, they are limited in that they view interpretation as linear, as shown in Figure 5.

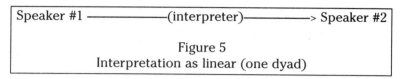

Figure 5
Interpretation as linear (one dyad)

In fairness to the current SL-to-TL models, they vary considerably. While earlier models saw the interpreter as a nonentity, similar to the machine metaphor, current process models have focused on the knowledge and decision-making involved in the interpreting process and have attempted to show the interpreter as part of the process with an impact on the interpretation. In this way, they differ greatly. However, they are similar in that the interpreting process is seen as linear, as involving one dyad with an interpreter between the two interlocutors. That is, the SL-to-TL models see the interpreter as someone who is either assumed to be invisible in the process (earlier models) or is seeking invisibility by striving for linguistic and cultural equivalence without detracting from the speaker's intended message (later models)[7]. However, in all of these models, the interpreter would focus on the *one dyad* created by the two speakers. Current research expands upon this view of interpretation by focusing on how the interpreter manages the interaction.

Current trends

Recent research in ASL-English interpretation has explored the interactive nature of the interpreted event. Roy (1992) explores turn-taking and the interpreter's decisions regarding who gets the floor when the interlocutors overlap. She uses an example of a successful interpretation to show that the interpreter used quite different strategies at different times. The interpreter either 1) stopped one or both of the speakers, 2) held the information and interpreted it at the end of a turn, 3) ignored a speaker completely, or 4) ignored a speaker and offered a turn to the other speaker (at the end of the current turn).

Roy shows that the decisions by the interpreter coincided with the expectations of the speakers, which in this case was a hearing college professor and a Deaf graduate student, and that is why the interpretation was viewed as successful by all parties — the professor, the student, and the interpreter. In sum, Roy shows that the interpreter participates in two dyads

— one dyad is composed of the interpreter and one speaker, and the other dyad is composed of the interpreter and the other speaker; that is, the interpreter negotiates meaning and turn-taking with each respective party, as shown in Figure 6. This approach, for example, would frame the miscommunication in Situation #2 (in which the hearing person interrupts the Deaf person) as an issue that would be dealt with within the interpreter - hearing speaker dyad, which is how the interpreter in this scenario handled the situation.

Stewart, Schein, and Cartwright (1998) have proposed an Interactive Model of Interpreting that is founded, in part, on the interpreting process models, but goes further to elaborate two-way interaction between the participants (through the interpreter). The Interactive Model of Interpreting makes use of environmental factors (physical and psychological factors) and sociolinguistic variables that are borrowed from the models of Colonomos (1992) and Cokely (1992), among others, and shows the interrelationship of these various factors. This Model considers the interpreter to be one of the participants (although a unique participant) and, thus, provides interpreters with an interactive model, similar to what we see in Figure 6 (adapted from Metzger, 1999, p. 181):

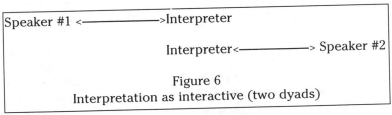

Speaker #1 <———————>Interpreter

Interpreter<———————> Speaker #2

Figure 6
Interpretation as interactive (two dyads)

Metzger (1999) explores the schemas (expectations regarding roles and the potential discourse) of the primary interlocutors and the interpreter in two medical interviews[8]. Metzger shows that each participant is acting in predictable ways based on their respective schemas and that each person's schema may be quite different from the other participants, and this has implications for the interaction. She also shows that the interpreter has more of an affiliation with the Deaf patient[9] than with the hearing healthcare professional(s). While these points raise valuable questions for the field (and have great implications for interpreters and potential research on schemas), our focus here is on how an interactional sociolinguistic approach can expand the schema of the interpreter. Metzger's work expands the view of interpreting to be three dyads (rather than a single dyad or two dyads), as shown in Figure 7 (adapted from Metzger, 1999, p. 24).

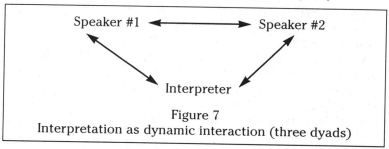

Figure 7
Interpretation as dynamic interaction (three dyads)

The contributions of this paper

This paper expands upon current conceptualizations of the interpreter's role and the interpreting process. The contributions of this paper are three-fold. It explores 1) the effect the interpreter's role as an interactional mediator has on the relationship between speakers, 2) the role of politeness in the interpreted interaction, and 3) a framework that interpreters can use to make decisions regarding politeness strategies.

3. The Nature of Face and Politeness Systems

This section defines two types of face needs and two politeness systems that affect interaction, and elaborates on their relative impact on power relations and the interpreting process. We first define positive and negative face needs, and then discuss two primary politeness systems and identify a third politeness system. We then discuss cultural differences and the implications of mismatched politeness systems on the relationship, the individual, and power relations. Finally, we revisit the three situations in light of face needs and these politeness systems.

Face needs and interactional sociolinguistics

Face, based on the early work of Goffman, can be defined as *a positive social value a person claims for oneself* or *making a good showing for one's group or oneself* (Goffman, 1967, p. 5). How this is accomplished varies from situation to situation, i.e., people use different strategies depending on the context in which they find themselves. However, people generally have two types of face needs, positive face needs and negative face needs, both of which are described briefly below.

First, a few words on interactional sociolinguistics are in order. Goffman's work (1967, 1974) on *self* and *face* as social or interactive constructs, and his notion of *framework*, are key components of interactional sociolinguistics. Goffman's notion of framework, a schema of interpretation of the events around us, provides a way of discussing how an individual perceives situations (e.g., social interactions). This notion elaborates how individuals "perceive, identify, and label" (Goffman, 1974, p. 21) a particular event using (usually) subconscious rules and, subsequently, imply a certain framework with his/her own response. Gumperz, (1982) whose work on *conversational inference* provides another key component of the interactional sociolinguistic framework[9]. Conversational inference "is the situated or context-bound process of interpretation, by means of which participants in an exchange assess others' intentions, and on which they base their responses" (Gumperz, 1982, p.153).

The interactional sociolinguistic framework is "grounded in a view of the self and what it does (e.g., make inferences, become involved) as a member of a social and cultural group and as a participant in the social construction of meaning" (Schiffrin, 1994, p. 101). In face-to-face interaction, "when listeners share speakers' contextualization cues, subsequent interactions proceed smoothly" (Schiffrin, 1994, p.100). That is, participants make inferences on interpersonal communication based on contextualized cues. Face and how face is dealt with, of course, play a crucial part in interaction.

Face actually presents a paradox between concern with one's *positive face*, "the person's right and need to be considered a normal, contributing, and supporting member of society" (Scollon & Scollon, 1995, p. 36) and concern with one's *negative face*, the individuality of the participant and his/her "right not to be completely dominated by group and social values, and to be free from the impositions of others" (Scollon and Scollon, 1995, p. 37). That is, face "consists of two specific kinds of desires ('face-wants') attributed by interactants to one another: the desire to be unimpeded in one's actions (negative face), and the desire (in some respects) to be approved of (positive face)" (Brown & Levinson, 1987, p. 13). As human beings, we communicate these two aspects of face simultaneously by using verbal and nonverbal cues (usually subconsciously) to let people know that we want approval, and, at the same time, to let people know that we do not want to be imposed upon in certain respects. Furthermore, all communication expresses face, i.e., "there is no faceless communication" (Scollon & Scollon, 1995, p. 38).

Politeness systems

Two primary politeness systems are used by speakers to address, or redress, one's face needs. The speaker's behavior may address either positive face needs, in which case the speaker uses the positive politeness system, or the speaker's behavior may address negative face needs, in which case the speaker uses the negative politeness system[11]. We will also discuss, below, a third politeness system that is a mixture of these two.

The positive politeness system

Positive politeness is used when the speaker attends to a person's positive face needs by affirming the wants/actions/values of this person (Brown & Levinson 1987, p. 101), as shown in Figure 8 below. Positive face behaviors communicate, "I want your positive face to be satisfied." The resulting behavior is free-ranging, e.g., familiar and joking behavior.

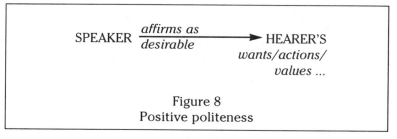

Figure 8
Positive politeness

An example of positive face at work is when someone is excited about sharing some new pictures with a group of close friends. Each person contributes to the discussion in a very familiar way, often (and most likely) joking with each other, with everyone feeling good about themselves and the interaction. In this example, everyone's positive face needs are being met.

The negative politeness system

Negative politeness is used when the speaker attends to a person's negative face needs. The purpose of negative politeness behaviors (Brown & Levinson 1987, p. 129) is to not hinder or impede the wants/actions/values of the person, as shown in Figure 9. Negative face communicates, "I will minimize the imposition of face threatening acts." The resulting behavior is specific and focused, e.g., respectful and unimposing behavior.

SPEAKER $\xrightarrow{\text{\textit{does not hinder}}_{\text{\textit{or impede}}}}$ HEARER'S
wants/actions/
values ...

Figure 9
Negative politeness

Negative politeness is most readily seen among people who, for whatever reason, want to respect each other's space, as in the case of meeting an important new person, such as a new boss or foreign dignitary. When meeting someone such as this, negative face wants are foregrounded, and one is on one's best behavior and tries to not impose. People in this situation generally follow social rules of decorum, i.e., negative politeness behaviors are used to attend to the negative face needs of the other person.

A third politeness system

There are situations in which a third politeness system is used. This third system is actually a mixture of the negative and positive politeness systems, in that one person uses one system and the other person uses the other system.

Scollon and Scollon (1995) introduce this third type of politeness system by first summarizing two types of symmetrical relationships. Positive politeness, or involvement (their term), is generally used with people of equal status, and is used when people are perceived as relatively close, such as with friends and close acquaintances. Negative politeness, on the other hand, may also be generally used with people of equal status, but is used when people are perceived as relatively distant. For example, this politeness system may be used with professional colleagues.

However, in an asymmetrical or hierarchical relationship, the participants are not of equal status and there is some assumed distance to their relationship, and the resulting strategies are mixed, assuming different behaviors on each person's part. The person in a higher position uses the positive politeness system (e.g., this person may be direct) and the person in the lower position uses the negative politeness system (e.g., this person is to be indirect). In short, the face needs of each person are different and correspond with the relative position of each. The person in a lower position attends (primarily) to the negative face needs of the person in the higher position, and the person in the higher position attends (primarily) to the positive face needs of the person in a lower position.

We return to these three systems when we discuss mismatches in politeness systems below. First, we discuss cultural differences between politeness systems.

Cultural differences

While it is impossible to assume that a whole cultural group uses the same politeness system, it is reasonable to talk about some underlying values and beliefs that make one system more prevalent than the other. However, we must always keep in mind that individuals make (usually unconscious) decisions about which politeness system to use based on how they perceive the social interaction and the face needs of the other interlocutor. That is, in addition to communicating information and intent, a person also communicates how s/he perceives the relationship. Is it symmetrical and close, symmetrical and distant, or asymmetrical and distant? The corresponding positive or negative politeness system will be used to convey how the relationship is perceived.

Scollon and Scollon (1995) address cultural differences in discourse systems between many Asian countries, which are hierarchical and based on the Confucian tradition, and many Western countries, which are egalitarian and based on the Utilitarian discourse system, which prefers "clarity, brevity, and sincerity" (Scollon and Scollon, 1995, p. 99). This dichotomy would predict a wider use of the asymmetrical or hierarchical discourse system in Eastern communities and a wider use of the symmetrical discourse system in Western communities. In actuality, one finds both systems "are used in both Asian and western communities... In other words, where people are in a close relationship to each other and of relatively equal status, in both east and west the normal pattern is the deductive pattern [representing the positive politeness system]" (Scollon & Scollon, 1995, p. 83), and they both use negative politeness in situations that call for deference.

For example, it is common for friends in Taiwan and Hong Kong to use the positive politeness system in conversations among friends, and it is common for friends in the United States to use the negative politeness system when requesting a big or embarrassing favor (such as asking to borrow a large sum of money). In this latter example, the focus is on massaging the relationship, in that "there would be an extended period of facework in which the would-be borrower would feel out the situation for the right moment in which to introduce his or her topic" (Scollon & Scollon, 1995, p. 83). So, while there may be cultural tendencies that are prevalent, the face needs within specific situations and within specific relationships determine which politeness system will be used.[12]

Now let us consider the implications of mismatched politeness systems between speakers. As human beings, we must, and do, draw inferences about meaning very quickly because of the ambiguous nature of language (Scollon & Scollon, 1995), and this is certainly the case with politeness strategies, i.e., we expect certain strategies to be used in certain situations. So what happens when there is a mismatch in strategies?

Implications of mismatched politeness systems

A mismatch in positive and negative politeness strategies may result in "bitterness and other negative attitudes when participants fail to come to agreement about their interpersonal relationship" (Scollon & Scollon, 1995, p. 87). Such a mismatch may affect face, power relations, and the treatment of interlocutors.

Goffman (1967) differentiates between acts that are in face and acts that cause a person to lose face. First, to be *in face* means the person feels assured that s/he is communicating as intended and feels confident; however, a person may also *lose face*:

Should he sense that he is in wrong face or out of

face, he is likely to feel ashamed and inferior because of what has happened to the activity on his account and because of what may happen to his reputation as a participant. Further, he may feel bad because he had relied upon the encounter to support an image of self to which he has become emotionally attached and which he now finds threatened. Felt lack of judgmental support from the encounter may take him aback, confuse him, or momentarily incapacitate him as an interacant... He may become embarrassed and chagrined; he may become shamefaced (Goffman, 1967, p. 9).

When speakers use different politeness strategies, there are also implications for the power dynamics in the interaction. *"When two participants differ in their assessment of face strategies, it will tend to be perceived as difference in power"* (Scollon & Scollon, 1995, p. 48).[13]

Here is an example of how a difference in politeness strategies can result in a change in the power dynamics: If both people use a positive or negative politeness system, then the assumption is that they see each other as equals, i.e., any power difference is minimized and they are primarily communicating how they perceive the relative closeness or distance of the relationship (reflecting how they are attending to the underlying face needs). However, if one person uses positive politeness and the other person uses negative politeness, the person using negative politeness is putting him/herself in a lower position. In essence, s/he is giving power to the other person because this positive politeness/negative politeness mix signals a hierarchical relationship (summarized from Scollon & Scollon, 1995, p. 48).

Differences in politeness strategies also indicate whether someone is a worthy member of a discourse group. Those who do not follow the expected norms may be treated as nonmembers. Those who follow the norms are considered normal and worthy of civilized treatment; those who do not may be considered less worthy, and may be denied the rights of other members of the group (Scollon & Scollon, 1995).

Differences in politeness strategies, then, may result in a person feeling embarrassed, may cause an unintentional change in the power dynamics, or may cast someone as a non-

member. All of these have serious consequences for interlocutors and for the conscientious interpreter who is interpreting and mediating the interaction. We will now return to
the three situations and see how an awareness of face needs
and politeness systems would affect how an interpreter would
handle the situations.

Face, politeness systems, and the situations

Now we return to the three situations and see how they
are interpreted given an interactional sociolinguistic
approach incorporating politeness strategies. In the first situation between the hearing supervisor and the new Deaf
employee, we see that the supervisor is using a positive
politeness strategy in that he asks a question directly of the
new employee. However, the supervisor is expecting the
employee to respond by using a negative politeness strategy,
but — as the interpreter knows — the employee answers the
question directly without the expected deference.

There are two crucial questions here: 1) Why are the two
choosing the same politeness strategy (i.e., positive politeness) even though their expectations differ (i.e., one is expecting an asymmetrical relationship and one is expecting a symmetrical relationship)? and 2) What would be the most appropriate way for the interpreter to handle the interpretation? I
will address each question in turn.

First, why is it that both the supervisor and the employee
are using the same politeness strategy? The hearing supervisor, it seems, is assuming a hierarchical relationship by asking
this direct question. When the Deaf employee responds with a
positive politeness strategy, he communicates that, in a sense,
he sees the supervisor as an equal. The supervisor's reaching
out to the Deaf employee in this way may well communicate
to the Deaf employee that the hearing supervisor wants to
deal with him as an equal. The employee, then, treats the
supervisor as someone in the in-group, and, in that case, the
best response is to use positive politeness. However, this is
not the expectation of the supervisor, who most likely expects
deference from the new employee.

This discussion leads to the second question: How should
the interpreter handle the situation? The interpreter really
has two clear choices: 1) the interpreter can do what was
done here and reflect the expectations of the hearing supervi-

sor (save face), or 2) the interpreter can reflect more literally how the speaker is expressing himself (not save face). In this second option, the interpreter would not mediate the interaction. Given the possible damage of interpreting literally, mediating the form of the message (direct communication) to what is appropriate in the TL and saving face seems the most appropriate. We can assume that the employee felt he was in face and was feeling good about this emerging relationship with his supervisor. If the interpreter ignores that for the sake of staying true to the form of the message, there is the potential of not meeting that person's face needs and possibly damaging the supervisor-employee relationship, neither of which was the employee's intent[14].

This is not to say that interpreters should always interpret to the expectations of the speaker(s) of the TL. However, the interpreter should take cues from the speaker and the interaction to determine the appropriate mediation. That is, the interpreter can watch for the person's intent in terms of interlocutors' goals, face needs, and what is being communicated about the relationship. The point, of course, is that it is crucial that the interpreter consider politeness strategies and their outcomes in situations such as this.

In the second situation, in which the hearing person interrupts, there seems to be some confusion about which politeness strategy is being used due to the pauses used by the interpreter (and, inadvertently, by the Deaf person). Short pauses indicate positive politeness and longer pauses indicate negative politeness. Silence communicates a subliminal system of norms and reflects what is perceived as enthusiasm, involvement, or positive politeness if there is little silence, and deference or negative politeness if there is more silence. So with these longer pauses, the hearing person may well assume a negative politeness strategy is being used, which is to say there is less involvement between the two speakers and it is his prerogative to speak.

Given that the miscommunication was due to the interpreting process and not a difference in politeness strategies (both speakers were, generally, using a positive politeness strategy), it seems clear that the interpreter has an obligation to save the face of the Deaf person and to repair this miscommunication by clarifying the intended politeness strategy. The interpreter in this case did just that by indicating there was a difficulty with the interpretation and by keeping the floor and rendering the interpretation.

In the third situation, involving a Deaf student's feedback in a graduate course, the Deaf student and the hearing students are using different politeness strategies. The Deaf student, we can assume, feels she is *in face* by giving direct feedback, using positive politeness. However, the other students are using a different discourse pattern, in which negative feedback is couched by making a positive comment first (with the relationship being foregrounded). The pattern of the hearing students is egalitarian and respectful and signals some distance, while the Deaf student's pattern is also egalitarian, but assumes less distance, i.e., her assumption is that direct comments should be the norm.

As with the Deaf employee and hearing supervisor, the Deaf student is using a discourse pattern which, in this case, is not in sync with the other students. The solution, then, is similar to the employee-supervisor situation. The interpreter again has two options — to interpret literally the way in which the student is expressing herself or to interpret in such a way that it fits the social situation, given the student's face needs.

In this case, the interpreter did the latter. Again, the consideration of how the interpretation is to be mediated must be made with consideration given to implications of face. In this case, the interpreter saves face for the student and conveys the information in such a way that it is taken in a positive light, as it is meant.

In each of these cases, we see that consideration of face provides the clearest explanation for what is happening in the interaction. While current metaphors and interpreting process models provide some guidance, it is only with the addition of an interactional sociolinguistic approach with the incorporation of politeness systems that an interpreter has an interpreting framework that is capable of accounting for the discourse differences in the scenarios and can make appropriate decisions in such situations.

Asymmetry in the interpreters' decisions

It is interesting to note how the interpreter handles the hearing students' comments in Situation #3. She does not reverse the order of the hearing students' comments even though the order of the Deaf student's comments are changed around, i.e., face considerations seem to occur in one direction. So why the apparent double standard? There are at least two reasons why the interpreter may not mediate face equally in both directions.

First, the interpreter may be functioning as an escort interpreter, which is commonly done when a foreigner visits another country. As an escort interpreter, the interpreter elaborates on the cultural customs of the country while functioning as an interpreter. In such a case, it would be more likely that the true nature of the Target Culture would be conveyed to the visitor and *more mediation* would occur *from* the Source Culture (the visitor). In other words, a more literal interpretation may be conveyed at times for the visitor's benefit, but it would be unusual for a literal interpretation to occur for the Target Culture's benefit, especially given the implications of face[15]. Again, this would be for the visitor's benefit regarding learning about the Target Culture. Functioning as an escort interpreter may account for why the interpreter saves face for the Deaf student, but not the hearing students in Situation #3.

Second, as a member of a minority group, the Deaf student is at a disadvantage and may more easily be discounted as an outsider. If the interpreter does not mediate the Deaf student's intent appropriately, the consequences could have serious repercussions on her ability to interact. The other students may take the student's comments in the wrong way and may be more reluctant to include her in the group. It, then, seems crucial for the interpreter to save face for the Deaf person (as appropriate) because of the student's minority status; this may not be the case for the hearing students.

Additionally, it is important to note that as the interpreter's working model is enhanced, so too are the interpreter's ethical considerations. Baker-Shenk (1992) shows that an interpreter's ethical considerations change when the interpreter's view of the interpreted interaction changes. That is, an interpreter functioning under a machine metaphor makes different ethical decisions than one who is functioning under a cultural mediator metaphor or ally metaphor. Likewise, with the field's increased understanding of the interpreted interaction, new ethical questions arise. Rather than assuming that only language is being conveyed or just language and culture are being conveyed, implications of mediating the interaction and the speakers' relationships add a new layer of ethical monitoring on the part of the interpreter. While the consideration of face is enlightening and increases awareness of this level of interaction, it also calls for more difficult decisions on the interpreter's part to determine the most appropriate way to reflect a speaker's politeness system in cross-cultural interaction.

4. Conclusion

This paper has shown that current models and metaphors do not provide adequate guidance for interpreters in face-to-face interaction. Specifically, three actual interpreting situations involving issues of face were approached from the perspective of different metaphors and interpreting process models, and then from the perspective of an interactional mediator metaphor — using an interactional sociolinguistic framework incorporating politeness. Only with the conceptualization provided with this last framework, which expands upon previous conceptualizations, is the interpreter able to 1) account for the discourse differences in these scenarios, 2) understand differences in politeness systems, and 3) have a framework that can guide him/her to reaching the most appropriate decision in such situations.

Some questions still linger and will require further research. These questions include the following: How does cross-cultural communication affect interlocutors' politeness strategies? What schemas do speakers and the interpreter(s) bring to cross-cultural communication? What are some strategies interpreters can use to effectively handle mismatches in politeness strategies? What strategies can interpreters use to attend to interlocutors' positive or negative face needs? What are the best methods of preparing student interpreters and professional interpreters for interpreting politeness strategies cross-culturally? Also, how do the face needs of interpreters affect the interpreted interaction?

Such research will benefit interpreters by increasing their understanding and expanding their conceptualization of the interpreted interaction. The consideration of politeness strategies is a step in the right direction and helps flesh out the interactional mediator metaphor further, in that it provides some clarification on these rule-governed, yet subconscious, systems that can make or break an interaction. The interpreter's role in mediating face appropriately is an important part of the interpreter's framework. Questions regarding face are crucial given there is no faceless communication and given that interpreters are the link in face between members of different cultural groups.

References

Baker-Shenk, C. (1986). Characteristics of oppressed and oppressor peoples: Their effect on the interpreting context. In M. McIntire (Ed.), *Interpreting: The art of cross cultural mediation* (59-71). Silver Spring, MD: RID Publications.

Baker-Shenk, C. (1992). The interpreter: Machine, advocate, or ally? In J. Plant Moeller (Ed.), *Expanding horizons* (pp. 119-140). Silver Spring, MD: RID Publications.

Brown, P., & Levinson, S. (1987). *Politeness: Some universals in language usage.* Cambridge, MA: Cambridge University Press.

Cokely, D. (1992). *Interpretation: A sociolinguistic model.* Burtonsville, MD: Linstok Press, Inc.

Colonomos, B. (1992). *The interpreting process.* Unpublished Manuscript.

Ford, L. (1981). The interpreter as a communication specialist. *Proceedings of the 3rd International Symposium of Interpretation of Sign Languages* (pp. 91-99). London: Royal National Institute for the Deaf.

Frishberg, N. (1990). *Interpreting: An introduction* (2nd ed.). Silver Spring, MD: RID Publications.

Goffman, E. (1967). On face work. *Interaction Ritual (pp. 5-46).* New York: Anchor Books.

Goffman, E. (1974). *Frame analysis.* New York: Harper and Row.

Gumperz, J. (1982). *Discourse strategies.* Cambridge, MA: Cambridge University Press.

Hoza, J. (1992). Doing the right thing: Interpreter role and ethics within a bilingual/bicultural model. In L. Swabey, (Ed.). *The challenge of the 90's: New standards in interpreter education* (pp. 101117). Conference of Interpreter Trainers.

Humphrey, J., & Alcorn, B. (1995). *So you want to be an interpreter? An introduction to sign language interpreting (2nd ed.).* Amarillo, TX: H & H Publishers.

Ingram, R. (1985). Simultaneous interpretation of sign languages: Semiotic and psycholinguistic perspectives. *Multilingua, 4,* 91102.

Kannapell, B. (1993). *Language choice Identity choice.* Burtonsville, MD: Linstok Press.

Lakoff, R. (1990). *Talking power: The politics of language.* Basic Books, a Division of Harper Collins Publishers.

McIntire, M, & Sanderson, G. (1995). Bye bye! Bi bi!: Questions of empowerment and role. In *A Confluence of Diverse Relationships: Proceedings of the Thirteenth National Convention of the Registry of Interpreters for the Deaf* (pp. 94-118). Silver Spring, MD: RID Publications.

Metzger, M. (1999). *Sign language interpeting: Deconstructing the myth of neutrality.* Washington, DC: Gallaudet University Press.

Page, J. (1993). In the sandwich or on the side? Cultural variability and the interpreter's role. *Journal of Interpretation, 6-1,* 107-125.

Roy, C. (1992). A sociolinguistic analysis of the interpreter's role in simultaneous talk in face to face interpreted dialogue. *Sign Language Studies, 74,* 21-61.

Roy, C. (1993). The problem with definitions, descriptions, and the role metaphors of interpreters. *Journal of Interpretation, 61,* 127-153.

Schiffrin, D. (1994). Interactional sociolinguistics. In *Approaches to discourse* (pp. 97-136). Cambridge, MA: Blackwell Publishers.

Scollon, R., & Wong Scollon, S. (1995). *Intercultural communication: A discourse approach.* Malden, MA: Blackwell Publishers.

Seleskovitch, D. (1994). *Interpreting for international conferences: Problems of language and communication (2nd revised ed.).* Washington, DC: Pen and Booth.

Stewart, D., Schein, J., & Cartwright, B. (1998). *Sign language interpreting: Exploring its art and science.* Needham, MA: Allyn and Bacon.

Witter-Merithew, A. (1986). Claiming our destiny. *Registry of Interpreters for the Deaf (RID) Views, 3,* (7), 12.

Footnotes

[1] The situations given in the paper are based on actual events; however, some of the specifics were altered to maintain the confidentiality of the participants.

[2] While these metaphors have been termed *models* in the literature, I use the term *metaphors* here (as does Roy, 1993). This is to distinguish these service metaphors, which seek to clarify an interpreter's role, from interpreting process models, which attempt to elaborate 1) the cognitive processes an interpreter undergoes and 2) considerations when engaging in interpretation. (For discussion of the underlying values of each metaphor, see Humphrey & Alcorn 1995 and McIntire & Sanderson 1995.)

[3] Although Baker-Shenk (1986) first referred to a *machine model* of ethical decision-making, this model has come to mean "the linguistic process of word-to-sign or sign-to-word, machine-like transliteration" (Baker-Shenk, 1992). Although these conceptualizations are much different (the first relating to a practitioner's behaving ethically as a machine [regardless of conception of the interpreting process] and the second referring to a rather literal interpretation), this second view has become so widespread, the term is used here in the second sense (see, for example, Witter-Merithew, 1986; Gish, 1990; Roy, 1993; Hoza, 1992).

[4] The field of ASL-English interpretation has referred to the metaphor unwittingly used in the early years of the field as *helper* (Witter-Merithew, 1986), but I do not address that metaphor here, as helper refers to the time in which interpreters were largely made up of benevolent, untrained volunteers who were the hearing friends or acquaintances of Deaf people, who took on the responsibility of interpreting. These interpreters worked without guidelines and, so, while this is of historical significance and, in fact, may have an impact on how interpreters work today (see, e.g., Gish, 1990), the only real consistency is that of care-taking, but such is beyond the scope of this paper, which is focusing on established metaphors that provide clear guidance in decision-making for interpreters.

5 Most of this research was phonologically, morphologically, and syntactically based, with little attention given to the nature of natural discourse, the focus of this paper.

6 These components of the process models are based on the early work of Seleskovitch (1994).

7 See Metzger (1999) for an analysis of the myth vs. reality of interpreter neutrality.

8 One is a roleplay situation and the other is an actual interpreted medical appointment.

9 She uses the interpreter's interpreter-initiated comments (interpreter initiated non-renditions) to show this affiliation, as almost all such comments are directed to the Deaf patient. She shows clearly that the interpreter is not a neutral party, and implores the field to stay current on research related to struggles used in interpreted interaction and to consider how it, as a profession, can assist speakers in understanding the role of the interpreter in interaction.

10 See Schiffrin (1994) for a summary of interactional sociolinguistics.

11 While scholars have used different terms for these politeness systems, I use the terms *positive politeness* and *negative politeness* from Brown and Levinson (1987) rather than the corresponding terms *involvement* and *independence*, respectively, from Scollon and Scollon (1995). The terms I have chosen here, I believe, provide for greater consistency between the politeness systems and the corresponding (positive or negative) face needs that each system addresses.

12 Page (1993) discusses the difference between individualistic, or low-context, cultures and collectivistic, or high-context, cultures. Individualistic cultures use a specificity pattern in which the *social role* a person is playing is trusted and distance is assumed; collectivistic cultures use a diffused, or holistic, pattern in which the *person* in the social role is trusted and personal involvement/connection is assumed. Each culture, then, would appear to prefer a certain politeness sys-

tem; however, this is not the case. Even though one may want to assume that collectivistic cultures would be more likely to use a positive politeness system and individualistic cultures would be more likely to use a negative politeness system, the situation is more complex than that. For example, the Japanese culture is high-context and collectivistic, but is more hierarchical, and American culture is low-context and individualistic, but is more egalitarian. It is the last feature (hierarchical vs. egalitarian) which seems to determine which politeness system is predominant. See Page (1993) for examples of how an American interpreter's role and a Japanese interpreter's role are perceived much differently. Specifically, the Japanese interpreter is expected to save face and promote harmony, which is not the case with the American interpreter.

13 Lakoff (1990) discusses the implications of language usage on power dynamics in everyday and professional life. She shows how people use special languages, or codes, (generally subconsciously) to achieve their ends, and argues that "Our every interaction is political" (p. 17) and "The savvy conversationalist can achieve power, as the inept can lose it, in the playing of the 'game'" (p. 49).

14 This does not mean that employees (or others) never intend to damage a relationship or that people do not lose face. The point, however, is that the speaker's intent, or goal, regarding the relationship and interlocutors' face needs are important considerations in determining an appropriate interpretation.

15 Two other possible factors may account for this asymmetry. First, the Deaf student may have a relative degree of bilingualism in ASL and English, and the interpreter may assume some English fluency on the Deaf student's part and may interpret more literally (see Kannapell, 1993 for a discussion of the relative bilingualism of deaf college students). Second, the interpreter may have second language limitations in ASL, which would impede full cultural mediation. However, these are less enlightening for our discussion here. By assuming the Deaf student's preference for ASL and the interpreter's bilingual, bicultural, and interpreting competence, we can focus on the issue at hand: asymmetry in decisions regarding face.

Journal of Interpretation

A Comparative Analysis of a Direct Interpretation and an Intermediary Interpretation in American Sign Language

Carolyn I. Ressler, M.A., CI and CT
Gallaudet University, Washington, D.C.

A Comparative Analysis of a Direct Interpretation and an Intermediary Interpretation in American Sign Language

Carolyn I. Ressler, M.A., CI and CT
Gallaudet University, Washington, D.C.

Abstract

Deaf relay interpreters and hearing intermediary inter-preters have been teamed up to provide interpreting services at many conferences and workshops. Although widely used, no research to date has been conducted determining what, if any-thing, the hearing interpreter must do differently while func-tioning in this intermediary role.

The goal of this research was to determine if there were dif-ferences between the direct interpretation, where the hearing interpreter was working directly from the source into the target language, and the intermediary interpretation, where the source message was "fed" to a Deaf interpreter. The hearing interpreter's direct interpretation of a source message was videotaped. This product was then compared to an intermedi-ary interpretation of that same text. Differences were noted in the areas of pausing, eye gaze, head nodding, the number of signs produced per minute, the use of fingerspelling versus signs, and in how clarifications were made.

Introduction

In years past, sign language interpreters have been viewed as simply having the responsibility of relaying messages from a source language into a target language. Although at first glance this task may seem to be a simple, straightforward one, much more is involved in this process. Inherent in this definition of interpreting is the notion of bilingualism. In order for a message to be communicated accurately from one language to the next, fluency in both languages is necessary. Yet, for many sign lan-guage interpreters, mastery of American Sign Language (ASL) as a second language is difficult to achieve. Not only does an aspiring interpreter have to learn the grammatical rules of the language as well as their applications, the interpreter is additionally challenged by the task of having to learn how to communicate through an entirely different mode or channel of message exchange. Whereas spoken languages make use of speech and auditory channels for sending and receiving communication, ASL relies upon a visual and manual mode of communication. This significantly increases the level of difficulty encountered when trying to master this language. This is the primary reason that, according to Charlotte Baker-Shenk (1986), "... the majority of hearing people who work as 'interpreters' are far from fluent in ASL" (p. 43). Baker-Shenk further states that the output that most interpreters produce is one resembling more of a transliterated product where the target message incorporates linguistic features from both English and ASL rather than a linguistically pure ASL product. From this understanding, the definition of sign language interpreting can be refined to include the task of extracting meaning and semantic intent of the source message from its form, and then formulating a target language message that expresses a near equivalent meaning according to the linguistic and cultural norms of the target population.

Nida and Taber (1974) captures the importance of meaning over form as such: " ... it is the content which must be preserved at any cost; the form, except in special cases, such as poetry, is largely secondary, since within each language the rules for relating content to form are highly complex, arbitrary and variable..." (p.104). Yet, for most interpreters whose second language is ASL, the form of the English utterance often takes precedence over content. As a result, pieces of the English form often appear in these second-language learners' ASL rendered product.

In an effort to remedy this situation, the notion of using Deaf relay interpreters, particularly at large conferences, has emerged. This idea provides a way to satisfy audience members desiring a culturally appropriate, accurate interpretation from English into ASL. At first thought, the concept of using a Deaf person to interpret a spoken English speech might seem somewhat preposterous. Yet logistically, it can be easily arranged; a spoken English text is channeled to a hearing interpreter who in turn signs, or "feeds," the message to the Deaf interpreter on stage. The Deaf interpreter then re-formulates the message and produces an ASL interpretation. It is hoped that, because of their native competencies in ASL and membership within the Deaf community, the Deaf interpreter will be better able to produce an interpreted message that is free of English-based grammatical structures and is similar in affect, meaning, and intent to the original spoken text. As described by Nancy Frishberg (1990) in her book *Interpreting: An Introduction*, interpreters who are Deaf have had a long history of interaction with other Deaf people. Although only 10 percent of Deaf children are born to Deaf parents, many Deaf children attend residential schools for the Deaf where ASL is the primary language of communication. As a result, Deaf people gain familiarization with a wide variety of communication and language styles including gestures, ASL, and other sign varieties. This exposure occurs often at all stages of development and growth. Because of this life-long exposure, Deaf interpreters often inherently possess necessary language competencies beneficial to the interpreting process.

Statement of the Problem

Although hiring Deaf relay interpreters seemingly resolves many concerns that arise when hearing interpreters work alone, Deaf interpreters are not being hired for conferences in the same numbers as their hearing colleagues. There are many reasons for this. Agencies and individuals hiring interpreters, for example, are often reluctant to cover costs and fees associated with the service. This becomes even more of a concern when additional interpreters are added, thereby doubling the expenses for the service.

Another factor contributing to the reluctance of hiring Deaf/hearing teams is that there is no evidence verifying the assumption that messages produced in ASL by Deaf relay interpreters are, in fact, more linguistically accurate and culturally appropriate than those produced by their hearing counterparts. Valid concerns are raised regarding the potential for information to be skewed and/or omitted when it is channeled through, not only one, but two interpreters.

Yet, above all these concerns, one of the most significant reasons why Deaf and hearing relay teams are not being hired is the difficulty in identifying qualified, experienced teams. The process of producing a direct interpretation when Deaf interpreters are not present is a complex one in and of itself. Extensive training is required for hearing interpreters before they are able to function in this role effectively.

In addition to being responsible for comprehending, processing, and communicating the source message to the target audience, the interpreter assumes numerous other responsibilities as well. S/he must assess the audience to determine the language needs. While in process, the interpreter must continually monitor audience comprehension based on explicitly stated and implicitly noted consumer feedback. The rate of flow of the source message must be controlled so as to ensure equivalency between it and the target message. Logistical concerns such as sufficient lighting, amplification, seating arrangements, and clear sight lines must also be handled. Continual adjustments are made by the interpreter as these areas are assessed and changes deemed necessary. These are just a few examples of the kinds of multiple tasks the interpreter is responsible for while producing a direct interpretation of the message.

The level of complexity is raised to even greater heights when Deaf and hearing interpreters are hired together. Not only do the above mentioned tasks have to be attended to, but in addition, the dynamics of the relationship within the Deaf/hearing team necessitates additional responsibilities. The "feed" language must be negotiated by the team. Depending on the bilingual skills of both interpreters involved, more or less processing of the source message may be necessary. The hearing interpreter must closely monitor the Deaf interpreter's comprehension of the "fed" message and adapt his/her work accordingly. Differences in the amount of processing time needed may require the hearing interpreter to alter his/her typical pace. Clarifications may need to be made between the hearing interpreter and the speaker, between the hearing interpreter and the Deaf interpreter, between the Deaf interpreter and the speaker, as well as between the audience and the interpreters and speaker.

The complexity of the task increases dramatically when Deaf and hearing interpreters work together. It is for this reason that few qualified teams exist. Training on how to work successfully in this capacity is rarely, if ever, offered. In fact, there are no guidelines or standards suggesting techniques for effectively interpreted exchanges with Deaf and hearing relay teams. Because no research currently exists on this topic whatsoever, it was to provide baseline data for the development of such standards that this research was undertaken.

Research Question

The intent of this descriptive case study was to determine if there are physically observable differences between a direct interpretation, where the hearing interpreter is working directly from the source into the target language, and an intermediary interpretation, where the source message is "fed" to a Deaf interpreter. Figure 1 graphically represents the research design.

The source language in this study was English. The top portion of this diagram represents the hearing interpreter producing an intermediary interpretation to a Deaf relay interpreter who then reformulates the message for the target audience. The bottom portion represents that same interpreter at a different time, directly interpreting the source message to the target audience. For the purposes of this research, the hearing interpreter's signed interpretations in the two different settings was compared and analyzed. Differences noted between the interpreter's product when working with a Deaf interpreter as opposed to when working independently will be discussed.

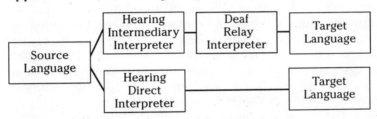

Figure 1
Research Design

Review of Literature

At the time of this study, no research had been done examining the relay interpreting process to determine effective strategies and techniques for relay teams. A review of existing research does, however, offer support for ASL based interpretations and provide information on effective strategies for successful interpretations for hearing interpreters.

Sign language interpreting as defined in the Introduction of this paper is a process by which messages from a source language are restructured and reproduced into a target language such that near equivalent meaning and affect are maintained. Studies by Fleischer (1975), Fleischer and Cottrell (1976) and Murphy and Fleischer (1977) investigated comprehension levels of Deaf consumers exposed to messages that were interpreted compared to those that were transliterated (messages signed in English word order by using manual signs for individual words and concepts). The first two studies, however, found no statistically significant differences in comprehension attributed to the differential treatments. However, individual student preferences for ASL or English based interpretations were not controlled for. The third study also did not control for language preference and its findings contradicted earlier research. In this study, the Deaf students involved scored significantly higher on tests when the material was presented to them in ASL as opposed to English. A flaw common to all three studies is that the material presented to the students was above their current knowledge base. Therefore, missed items on the administered tests may be a result of the subjects' lack of familiarity with the topic as opposed to language comprehension levels. In addition, the interpreters had the opportunity to rehearse the lecture material in advance. This is considered a luxury and rarely occurs outside of the testing environment. Finally, students' comprehension levels were based on questions they responded to in written English form. In light of the fact that English functions as a second language for many Deaf students, an additional literacy factor was introduced into the study. A study conducted by Livingston, Singer and Abrahamson (1994) attempted to correct for earlier research design flaws. In this study, Deaf students were grouped according to stated language preferences into two groups, those preferring ASL and those preferring English based signing. Depending on which group they were in, subjects viewed either an ASL interpretation or transliteration of a 10-minute videotape. Comprehension levels were determined by responses to questions regarding the material in the message. Both the questions and answers were communicated in ASL. Results indicated that subjects achieved higher scores when the material was presented in ASL rather than transliterated. This was found to be true even for students who expressed a preference for a transliterated message but received the material in ASL. From this, Livingston, Singer and Abrahamson (1994) concluded that

"ASL works better for all Deaf students in mainstreamed college classes" (p. 1).

As indicated by these studies, there are advantages to interpreted messages over those that are transliterated. Research
has been conducted in an effort to determine what interpreters
must do in order to produce a clear and accurately interpreted
message. For example, Llewellyn-Jones (1981) investigated the
effect that interpreted messages had on the amount of information understood by the Deaf consumers. Successful interpretation that resulted in consumer comprehension occurred
when the meaning of the source message was extracted and
restructured into the target language. It was only when this
occurred that consumers were able to understand the material. Cokely (1992) went one step further to examine errors that
result in miscues or deviations from the source message. He
identified five significant types. Each of these is defined by
Cokely (pp. 74-75) in the following manner:

1) Omissions: Information that is found in the source language
that is absent from the target language message.

2) Additions: Information that is not intended or produced in
the source message that appears in the target message interpretation.

3) Substitutions: Information contained in the source message
that has been replaced by information in the interpretation
that is at variance with the intent of the source language message.

4) Intrusions: Source language syntactic structures in the interpretation that result in a transliteration of the source message
rather than an interpretation. These result in an adherence to
the syntax and lexical semantics of the source language.

5) Anomalies: Utterances that are meaningless or confused and
cannot be accounted for by other miscue types.

He found the number of resulting miscues (errors) produced
in the target language to be a direct result of the interpreter's
target language incompetence among other factors. Cokely's
research further concluded that simply transferring the form of

the source language without regard for its meaning resulted in linguistic difficulties for the consumers. From these studies, several conclusions can be drawn. Effective interpretations are produced when the interpreter is, first, able to extract the meaning from the form of the source message and, second, able to reproduce it in the target language.

Even for qualified, experienced interpreters who are fluent in both English and ASL, unfamiliar and subtle nuances of the language can impede their ability to produce native-like interpretations in ASL. For example, a study by Zimmer (1989) examined the interpretation of an interactive speech event between two hearing and one Deaf individual. Exchanges made between the two hearing women were compared to those between the hearing and Deaf women. Although issues of comprehension and message equivalence were not of concern in this study, significant differences were observed when comparing the interpreted and non-interpreted exchanges. These differences occurred at the discourse level in the areas of pauses, pause-filling devices, and repair strategies. As evidenced by this study, even when the language factor is not of concern, specific in-group norms that are inherently understood by members of a culture play an important role in the communication process. Winston (1990) attributes these subtle non-native errors made by interpreters to "accents" they possess. She narrowed the accented features into two categories: those pertaining to articulation problems (handshape, movement, location, and palm orientation) and those she refers to as gestalt problems (use of appropriate amounts of space, head nods, head and body rotation, eyebrow movement, eye gaze, mouth movements, rhythm, and pacing). Through an intense training process, Winston was able to show a marked decrease in the "thickness" of the interpreter's accents in the study. Unfortunately, the amount of time and the materials necessary for this type of accent reduction training does not make this remedy one easily attained.

In summary, although sign language interpreting has been occurring for decades, it has only been within the last 10 years that there has been an interest in the study and analysis of the interpreting process. In general terms, interpreting research conducted has indicated better comprehension levels by Deaf individuals when ASL based interpretations were produced. Interpreters fluent in both ASL and English are more capable of taking the source language message and reproducing it into the target language with fewer miscues occurring than interpreters who are less bi-lingual. However, even when an interpreter is competent in ASL, unfamiliar, subtle language nuances may never be acquired by an interpreter learning ASL as a second language. "Hearing accents" are noted to exist that result in non-native errors being produced by hearing interpreters. Although research to date indirectly supports the need for Deaf relay interpreters who are native ASL users, Deaf/hearing working teams are rarely seen. Because research analyzing this intermediary interpreting process is not available, there is no data that explains or investigates the effectiveness of Deaf/hearing interpreting teams.

Methodology

Subjects
Currently in the United States, few experienced, conference-level Deaf/hearing relay teams exist. One of these teams was geographically local and therefore was selected to produce the data for this research. Information obtained prior to the start of this research indicated that both of the interpreters had been certified by the Registry of Interpreters for the Deaf at the highest level. The Deaf interpreter had been certified for 10 years and holds a Reverse Skills Certificate (RSC). The hearing interpreter had been certified for 13 years and holds a Comprehensive Skills Certificate (CSC), a Specialized Certificate in Legal Interpreting (SC:L), and a Certificate of Interpretation (CI). The Deaf interpreter has been interpreting professionally for 15 years and the hearing interpreter for 14 years. Their experience working together as a team in this type of a setting in addition to their level of certification and accessibility made them suitable subjects for the purposes of this study.

Data Collection
It was important for the interpreters to have audibly clear, unambiguous stimulus materials to work from in the laboratory setting. The Department of Interpreting and Linguistics at Gallaudet University has professionally produced videotapes of spoken English dialogues made for the purpose of simulating live spoken presentations. These tapes were produced for

training interpreters and, as a result, have been determined a close replica of a true-to-life presentation.

The interpreters were asked to interpret one of these video-taped spoken English monologues. The tape was approximately 16 minutes long. During the videotaping, the interpreters were seated such that they were facing one another so as to allow direct, clear communication between the two of them. Their interpreted products were videotaped in a split screen format so that both interpreters' outputs could be seen simultaneously.

In a natural setting, the interpreters would typically have access to the speaker's notes or outline to help them prepare for the interpreting task. This information alerts the interpreter to any specific jargon or complex terminology the speaker may cover during his/her remarks. In an effort to simulate this in the laboratory, a summary of the English text was given to them outlining the key points of the presentation. They were instructed that they were to work as if they were interpreting for an audience primarily made up of ASL users attending a large conference.

A few months later, the hearing interpreter was then asked to return and interpret the monologue a second time. It was necessary to allow several months to pass before asking the interpreter to repeat the interpretation. Had the interpreter been asked to sign the taped message immediately following the first taping, she may have retained some of the information discussed on the video. Having this prior knowledge to work from she may have been able to predict upcoming information and adjust her product accordingly. In order to minimize this learning affect, it was necessary to wait several months before re-taping the piece a second time. The interpreter was given the same outline and instructions; however, this time she was asked to work independently, rather than as a "feed" in a relay team. Her direct interpretation was videotaped.

Analytical Process

It was important to have a native user of ASL assist in the analysis of the data and, therefore, a native ASL Deaf linguist was hired to assist with the transcriptions of the hearing interpreter's signed products. The beginning 10 minutes of the interpretation was not analyzed so as to give the interpreter(s) adequate time to become accustomed to the speaker, pace, and content. Each ASL sign produced by the hearing interpreter after the initial 10 minutes was described using an English gloss and supplemented with conventional symbols used for transcribing signed texts. These individual sign glosses were then arranged into ASL sentences (see Appendix A for example of direct interpretation transcriptions and Appendix B for example of intermediary interpretation transcriptions). A general comparison of the two transcribed interpretations and videotapes was conducted by the researcher and linguist to determine if differences between the two existed. In an effort to make this determination, it was assumed that, if variations between the two interpretations existed, they would fall into certain categories of linguistic features. These categories include such indicators as sign choices, pausing/timing, fingerspelling versus production of a sign, eye gaze signals, and other aspects of the language. These particular categories were selected because they are most often referred to when describing prominent features of ASL and when comparing differences in direct interpretations. These features and others in the two interpretations were then observed and compared.

Results

The process of writing an English gloss for a visual language such as American Sign Language has not yet been perfected. For this reason, the five minutes of transcriptions produced for each of the two interpretations required a total of nearly 100 hours of work on the part of this researcher and the Deaf linguist. Each frame of the videotape was frozen on the television screen so that manual and non-manual information could be recorded. Individual signs were broken down into movements produced by the right hand and movements produced by the left hand. After viewing both of the interpretations and reviewing the recorded data, several prominent, observable differences between the two interpretations became evident. Once these differences were noted, the videotapes were further analyzed. Again, by viewing each still-frame of the videotapes, these particular features were documented and described. These differences fell into the following six categories: 1) pausing, 2) eye gaze, 3) head nods, 4) the number of signs produced per minute, 5) fingerspelling versus signs and, 6) clarifications between the two interpreters. Findings in each of these areas are presented and discussed below.

Pausing

Spoken messages, as well as signed messages, are typically fragmented and discontinuous in their natural form. These hesitations and stops in the flow of spoken and signed messages are often referred to as pauses. Pausing also occurs within the interpreting process. The data collected on the videotape, however, indicated differences in how long and how often the interpreter paused in the two interpretations. In an effort to document and describe the pausing differences, all of the pauses used by the interpreter were noted and timed in the targeted sections of each videotape. These pauses occurred in one of two forms and thus were categorized into two distinct types: pauses and pause/holds.

Instances when the interpreter was not actively engaged in signing and her hands were at a rest position are referred to in this research as pauses in the interpretation. Research by Cokely (1992) suggests that these pauses are often purposefully and strategically produced by the interpreter so that s/he can lag behind the speaker. This lag time is spent understanding and processing the incoming source message before producing the target interpretation.

Pause/hold is the term coined by this researcher to describe specific times when the final position of a sign was held beyond what would seem to be standard length of time before moving on to produce the subsequent sign. The point of distinction between a pause and a pause/hold is whether or not the hands are at rest. In a pause, the final sign is produced and then the hands typically lower to a rest position in front of the body. However, in a pause/hold, the end position and handshape of the last sign produced remain in place and are held for an extended period of time before the production of the subsequent sign occurs. Although, as mentioned above, pauses in an interpretation have been noted in only a few studies, nowhere in existing research has mention been made of the pause/hold phenomena observed in the data collected for this study.

Analysis of the targeted segment of the direct interpretation video revealed that, of the total running time of 343 seconds, a total of 8 pauses and 16 pause/holds occurred. Each of these was timed with a stop watch to determine the duration. In the direct interpretation, the interpreter paused (without a hold) for a total of 11.80 seconds. In addition, for 34.46 seconds, the interpreter paused while holding the last sign produced.

Therefore, of the 343 seconds of video examined, in 46.26 seconds, or 13.5% of the time on task, the interpreter was pausing with or without hold.

The intermediary interpretation was also examined for the number of and length of pauses and pause/holds. Pauses (without hold) occurred 17 times lasting a total of 45.49 seconds, and pause/holds occurred 30 times amounting to 64.61 seconds. In this interpretation, the interpreter was pausing with or without hold 32.1% of the time.

In addition to interpreter pauses, the speaker also naturally paused between thoughts or ideas, or as he was gathering his thoughts. In the targeted segment, speaker pauses were determined by timing with a stopwatch the length of time between the last word spoken before a pause and the beginning of the following utterance. All pauses 0.80 seconds or longer were noted and timed. Of the 343 total seconds of data analyzed, the speaker paused 45 times for a total of 51.73 seconds. In this segment then, the speaker was not speaking but rather pausing approximately 15% of the time. Table 1 summarizes the pauses (P) and pause/holds (P/H) for both interpretations and for the speaker.

Table 1
Pauses (P) and Pause/Holds (P/H)

	# of Pauses	# of Pauses/ Holds	Total P time (sec)	Total P/H time (sec)	% of time P and/or P/H
Direct Interpretation	8	16	11.8	34.46	13.40%
Intermediary Interpretation	17	30	45.49	64.61	32.10%
Speaker	45	NA	51.73	NA	15.10%

Eye Gaze

Eye gazing refers to instances when an individual's eyes are directed towards a person, object, or location in space. Movements of the eyes serve particular functions in daily interactions. Kendon (1967) identified four functions of eye gazing. These function are 1) cognitive—individuals tend to look away when they are having difficulty encoding information; 2) monitoring—individuals may look at the person they are addressing to indicate the conclusion of thought units and to check for alertness and reactions; 3) regulatory—individuals may look at a person in an effort to demand or suppress a response; and 4) expressive—individuals can use eye gaze to express a certain degree of involvement or arousal. In addition to these functions, eye gazes in ASL also play an important role in the grammatical structure of the language. Eye gazes are used, for example, to establish referents in space, mark pronouns, and indicate emphasis, as well as other grammatical functions. Typically, an interpreter's eye gaze will also shift between several target points throughout a direct interpretation. In order to determine if eye gaze behavior was different in an intermediary interpretation, the videotaped data of both interpretations were analyzed.

Although it is very difficult to determine precisely where the interpreter's eyes are focusing, six general locations were noted in the tapes. These locations are not mutually exclusive and are as follows: up, down, right, left, audience, and classifier. Most are self explanatory with the exception of the "classifier" and "audience" locations.

Eye gazes listed as being at "classifier" locations referred to instances when the interpreter's eyes locked in on the sign classifier being produced. Classifiers are common in the grammatical structure of ASL. They are particular signs that represent whole categories of words and, in addition, also are used to indicate size, shape, or movement of objects. The structure of ASL necessitates eyes gaze to be directed at the classifier when it is produced by the signer. For this reason, it was necessary to indicate eye gaze at the classifier location when observed.

The audience location indicates that the interpreter made direct eye contact with the audience. In the direct interpretation, the audience was the camera and the individual operating the equipment. For the intermediary interpretation, an eye gaze listed as audience in the glossed transcription refers to instances when the interpreter made direct eye contact with the Deaf interpreter.

Examination of the interpreter's eye gaze in the direct interpretation indicated that the interpreter's eyes naturally shifted between the various locations in space. Particular attention was given to the location of the eyes during pauses and pause/hold times. Of the eight pauses observed in the direct interpretation, during six of those pauses the interpreter's eyes were gazing downward. In one instance the interpreter's eyes were gazing upward and in the other to the right. In this segment, 16 pause/holds were noted. During nine of those pause/holds, the interpreter's eyes were gazing downward. Although eye gazes for the remaining seven pause/holds were found to be directed towards various other locations, eye gazes directed at the audience did not occur. In summary, for both pauses and pause/holds in the direct interpretation, the interpreter's eyes were typically observed to be directed downward. Although eye gazes were noted in other locations, the interpreter's eyes were never observed to be directed at the audience during a pause or a pause/hold time.

Eye gaze results were very different in the intermediary interpretation. During the 17 pause times in this interpretation, the interpreter's eyes were primarily fixed directly on the Deaf interpreter (noted as the "audience" location). Of the total 17 pauses, the interpreter's eyes were found to be directed at the audience 12 times, at the audience/down location twice, and at the audience/right location twice. On only one occasion did the interpreter pause while looking directly downward and not at the audience. Analysis of eye gazes during the pause/hold times produced similar results. Of the 30 pause/holds observed, the interpreter's eye gaze locations were noted as follows:

> Audience (Deaf interpreter) - 20 occurrences
> Audience/Down - 3 occurrences
> Audience/Right - 2 occurrences
> Audience/Left - 1 occurrence
> Downward - 3 occurrences
> Right - 1 occurrence

In summary, in the intermediary interpretation, during both pause times and pause/hold times, the interpreter primarily made direct eye contact with the Deaf interpreter, whereas analysis of eye gaze in the direct interpretation revealed that, although the interpreter's eyes were noted in various locations, in general, they were directed downward. In addition, in the direct interpretation, the interpreter's eyes were never observed to be directed at the audience during a pause or a pause/hold time.

Head Nodding

ASL incorporates head nods as part of the grammatical structure of the language. Grammatical head nods in ASL serve as indicators of affirmative statements, distinguish one sentence type from another, and also function as a means for adding emphasis to spoken statements. In both interpretations, these grammatical head nods were noted. In the direct interpretation, two typical grammatical head nods were observed. Both were accompanied by a sign in an effort to emphatically communicate the spoken message. Likewise, in the intermediary interpretation, three similar grammatical head nods were observed.

In addition to the standard head nodding described above, a different type of head nodding was also observed in the intermediary interpretation only. These head nods can best be described as being monitoring head nods since they are not a necessary part of the source or target messages and were only produced as a monitoring technique. In the intermediary interpretation, 10 of these monitoring head nod types were observed. These head nods were noted as occurring only during times when the hearing interpreter paused while holding a sign (pause/hold times). In addition, in each of these pause/hold instances where head nodding occurred, the interpreter's eye gaze was focused directly at the audience (Deaf interpreter) location. In each of these instances, during the pause that occurred after the hearing interpreter had fed a portion of the spoken message to the Deaf interpreter, the hearing interpreter watched and nodded as the Deaf interpreter produced in ASL the fed information. Once the information had been successfully interpreted by the Deaf interpreter, the hearing interpreter ceased the nodding behavior and continued on with the feed process. The head nods in these instances were not required in order to communicate the source message but only occurred as a monitoring strategy.

In summary, grammatical head nods were observed to exist in both the direct and intermediary interpretations. No clear differences were noted in the frequency or function of these nodding behaviors. However, an additional type of head nodding was noted in the intermediary interpretation that was not present in the direct interpretation. These head nods functioned as a means by which the fed message was monitored by the hearing interpreter while the Deaf interpreter produced the target message

Signs/Words Per Minute

Using a stop watch, the number of words spoken per minute by the speaker and the number of signs produced per minute by the interpreter were calculated. False starts made by the speaker and the interpreter were eliminated and only the actual signs and words were counted. In the 5 minutes and 43 seconds of the video segment analyzed, the speaker spoke 949 words or an average of 166 words per minute. Likewise, the number of signs produced per minute in the direct and intermediary interpretation were also computed. In the direct interpretation, approximately 611 signs were produced by the interpreter in the target segment. This averages out to approximately 107 signs produced per minute. Only 500 signs were noted in the intermediary interpretation resulting in approximately 88 signs used per minute. It is important to note with the intermediary interpretation that, on several occasions, the hearing interpreter made comments directed to the Deaf interpreter for clarification purposes. These comments, although outside of the source message, are included in the above calculated signs per minute. If, however, the signs produced in the dialogue between the two interpreters were to be excluded from the calculation, the total adjusted number of signs would be approximately 473 or an average of 83 signs per minute. A summary of the signs/words per minute is provided in Table 2.

Table 2
Signs/Words per Minute

	Total # of words/signs	Avg. words/signs per minute
Speaker	949	166
Direct Interpretation	611	107
Intermediary Interpretation	473	83

In summary, more words per minute were spoken by the speaker than signs produced by the interpreter in the direct and intermediary interpretations. When comparing only the interpreted products, the interpreter produced an average of 24 signs more per minute in the direct interpretation than was produced in the intermediary interpretation.

Fingerspelling Versus Signs

Although there are certain English words that can be finger-spelled when interpreting into ASL, interpreters typically have the option of using a sign or cluster of signs to communicate an intended concept. Both of the videos were examined to determine if the use of fingerspelling occurred more frequently in one than in the other. The interpreter fingerspelled words 21 times in the direct interpretation and 29 times in the intermediary interpretation. Although this initially did not seem to indicate a significant difference between the two products, differences were noted in the actual number of individual words fingerspelled. In the direct interpretation, the interpreter fingerspelled only seven different words. Several of these words though were fingerspelled repeatedly. For example, although the English word "door" was spelled out five times by the interpreter it was counted as only one occurrence of fingerspelling. In the intermediary interpretation, 20 different words were fingerspelled to the Deaf interpreter with only a few being spelled more than one time. Also, when comparing the actual words that were fingerspelled in both interpretations, only one word, "airbag," was fingerspelled by the interpreter in both situations.

Clarifications

In order for interpretation accuracy to be achieved, it was necessary for the Deaf and hearing interpreters to dialogue with one another throughout the course of the spoken message. In that the hearing interpreter is working alone in a direct interpretation, no such dialogue can occur. Three instances of clarification dialogue were observed in the intermediary interpretation. Each of them occurred for different reasons. The first dialogue was initiated by the hearing interpreter when she realized erroneous information had been fed to the Deaf interpreter. The source and target messages were as follows:

> Source Message: "I will give you the bad news and then end with the good news."
> Fed Message: "PRO-1 START WITH GOOD NEWS . . ."
> (Backtranslation: I will start with the good news . . .")

Once the hearing interpreter realized the error, a lengthy pause occurred followed by an explanation, intended for the Deaf interpreter only, correcting the mis-fed information.

The second dialogue was much shorter in length. The hearing interpreter fed the number "150,000" to the Deaf interpreter. The need for clarification in this instance was prompted by the Deaf interpreter who through the use of subtle, non-coded facial grammar quickly asked for repetition of the number from the hearing interpreter. The number was repeated and the process continued.

The third interpreter dialogue took place towards the end of the session. Due to the hearing interpreter's lag time, the source tape ended before the information was entirely fed to the Deaf interpreter. The hearing interpreter wanted to turn off the machine and rather than simply doing so, alerted the Deaf interpreter to the fact that the tape was over and the message remaining to be fed was nearly completed.

Dialogue between the Deaf and hearing interpreters was observed to have occurred in the intermediary interpretation only. These discussions were opportunities for the interpreters to clarify misunderstood and mis-fed information. Requests for clarifications were initiated by both interpreters for several different reasons.

Discussion and Conclusions

Results from this study indicate that clear differences between a direct and an intermediary interpretation exist. These differences have been noted in, but are not limited to, the areas of pausing, eye gaze, head nodding, signs per minute, fingerspelling, and clarifications. Speculations as to how and why these differences occur can result in a clearer understanding of the Deaf/hearing interpreting team process.

Pausing was one area where significant differences appeared between the two interpretations. First though, it is important to compare the percentage of time the speaker paused (15.1%) with the percentage of time the interpreter paused in the direct interpretation (13.4%). These numbers would indicate that the speaker paused slightly more time overall than the interpreter did. Cokely (1992) found this to be true as well in his temporal analysis of interpreter and speaker pause times. He determined that interpreters consciously make use of speaker pauses to reduce the portion of time simultaneously listening and processing the source for understanding and producing the target message. This then would affirm the findings of this research when the speaker pauses are compared to the direct interpretation pauses. However, a very different phenomenon exists when introducing a Deaf interpreter into this process. A significantly higher percentage of time (32.1%) is spent by the intermediary interpreter either pausing or in a pause/hold state. Analysis of the data collected offers plausible insight into why and how this may occur.

The data related to eye gaze indicate that, in a direct interpretation, the interpreter's eyes are averted downward during the majority of the pause and pause/hold times. The downcast eye gaze appears to reflect a listening and processing state. The interpreter seems to be making use of this time by intently listening and comprehending the incoming source message. The same is not true for pause and pause/hold eye gazes in the intermediary interpretation. During these pauses, the interpreter's eyes are fixed on the Deaf interpreter ensuring comprehension of the fed message, watching for requests for clarifications, and checking for accuracy. This monitoring of the fed message is also evident through the observation of the greater number of head nod occurrences. The number of head nods occurring during the pause/hold times while the interpreter's eyes were directed to the Deaf interpreter would seem to reinforce the idea that the hearing interpreter is checking for accuracy, monitoring comprehension, and providing feedback to the Deaf interpreter. The necessity of this type of monitoring in a fed interpretation was made evident as clarifications were made and dialogue took place between the two interpreters. It was imperative, for example, that the hearing interpreter be watching the Deaf interpreter closely when the source message was mis-fed. The hearing interpreter made clear indications that the error was made in the fed information, re-stated the information correctly, and then watched to make sure the intended concept was delivered. Likewise, later in the interpretation the hearing interpreter was asked to restate a number per the request of the Deaf interpreter. This again supports the finding that more time is spent regularly monitoring the fed message and the final message as produced by the Deaf interpreter. All of these factors, the fixed eye gaze, increased and directed head nods, and dialogue over clarifications, substantiate the necessity for the increased pausing and pause hold times in intermediary interpreting settings.

Now, the question of "How?" arises. If the hearing interpreter is managing the exact same source message in both settings, how can the total time spent pausing be nearly tripled in the intermediary interpretation and still achieve source/target message equivalence? The data analyzed suggests several plausible strategies initiated by the hearing interpreter to achieve equivalence despite the increased pause time.

The first of these proposed strategic solutions to the question of message equivalence in spite of increased pause time can perhaps be found in the number of signs produced per minute. As described earlier, results indicate that on average the interpreter in the feed position produced 24 fewer signs per minute than when interpreting that same information for the direct interpretation. The total average number of signs per minute (107) produced when the Deaf interpreter was not present parallels results found in Cokely's (1992) research. Cokely reported an unadjusted average rate of 100.45 signs per minute being produced by interpreters in direct interpretation settings. The finding that only 83 signs per minute occurred in the fed interpretation seems to reflect an alternative means by which source information is being relayed to the Deaf interpreter. One technique the interpreter in the feed setting used to reduce the total number of signs was to fingerspell certain concepts instead of using a cluster of signs to communicate the concept. Typically in direct interpretations, interpreters utilize expansion techniques to communicate ideas and concepts rather than simply fingerspelling the English word. These expansions require several signs to be strung together in such a way so that the conceptual meaning behind the single English word is understood. Often in the intermediary interpretation, the interpreter chose to spell out specific words as opposed to using an expansion technique. The expansion of the concept was then left up to the Deaf interpreter to produce. For example, the source message introduced the concept of "automatic restraint systems." There is no single ASL sign that would communicate with conceptual accuracy this term. In the intermediary interpretation, the hearing interpreter fingerspelled the words, "automatic restraint." However, in the direct interpretation the interpreter expanded the concept by signing, "PRO-rt HAVE CL:belt shoulder CL:belt waist UNDERSTAND+ CL:belt shoulder ATTACH-dir fs:door CL:U on IX, sliding outwards, then back to IX" Clearly from this one example, the length of time needed to fingerspell the term as opposed to produce the expanded sign cluster is much less. Significant amounts of time could be saved by the hearing interpreter fingerspelling terms and allowing the expansions to occur through the Deaf interpreter. The time conserved here then could be used in pauses so that monitoring, clarifications, and accuracy checking could occur, thus accounting for the increased pause and pause/hold times in intermediary interpretations.

Limitations of the Study

Although the findings of this study reveal some indications of differences between direct and intermediary interpretations, there are limitations to the results reported. Most noticeable is the fact that data collected came from only one Deaf/hearing relay team. Results observed may be specific to this particular team and not generalizable to other teams in other settings. Sadly, not many teams are trained and available for this type of analysis. Analysis of data collected for other Deaf/hearing teams may help to support or refute results obtained in this study.

In addition, the data were collected in a nonnaturalistic setting. The interpreters were videotaped in a laboratory setting and did not have access to what might be considered a live audience. This can affect the interpreters' work in that they were not able to incorporate feedback from audience participants and accordingly adjust their interpretation as is typically done. Taping done in "live" settings would result in more naturally occurring products.

Although several months transpired between the first taping of the intermediary interpretation and the second direct interpretation, the hearing interpreter had heard the source material before producing the direct interpretation. Although the intermediary interpretation could be considered a "cold" interpretation, the direct interpretation was not. This raises a problem because, despite the passage of time between the two tapings, some of the source message may have been retained by the hearing interpreter. It is often the case that information heard a second time is easier to interpret because initial understanding and processing have already taken place during the first hearing. Ideas and concepts are more familiar the second time around allowing the interpreter to be more prepared. In real-world settings, interpreters rarely have the luxury of hearing a source message in its entirety before producing an interpretation for the target audience. Another factor that may have influenced the data collected for the direct interpretation is that the hearing interpreter had already observed the Deaf interpreter's target interpretation during the intermediary process. The Deaf interpreter's style and language use may have influenced the sign choices and signed concepts of the hearing interpreter in her direct interpretation.

Although the hearing interpreter had previously heard the spoken text and had seen the Deaf interpreter's rendition of the spoken message prior to producing the direct interpretation, major differences between the two products still existed. Had the taping been done in the opposite order (direct interpretation before intermediary interpretation), the hearing interpreter would not have had the benefit of seeing the material modeled by the Deaf interpreter. Yet, even with the fact that the hearing interpreter may have retained and incorporated some of the Deaf interpreter's work into the direct interpretation, major differences between the two interpretations still existed. It can be presumed that reversing the order of the tapings would only magnify the differences observed here because the hearing interpreter would then be working without any language modeling from which to draw.

Not having access to high-tech equipment also may have resulted in some skewing of the data collected. Optimally, equipment that recorded and displayed minutes, seconds, and tenths of seconds digitally on the tape should have been used. Greater accuracy in the calculations of pause times, pause/hold times, words/signs per minutes, and other temporal aspects could have been achieved had this type of equipment been used. Calculations based on data recorded through timings with the stop watch indicated clear and distinct differences in the two interpretations. Although some minor variances in the numerical data collected may be noted if a more precise data collection technique were used, major variances in overall results and noted differences would most likely not be found.

Implications and Areas of Suggested Future Study

No research has been conducted to date studying the intermediary interpretation process. As result, Deaf/hearing interpreter teams are often brought together to complete a task that neither has received instruction on performing. Although typically hearing interpreters have experience working independently in providing a direct interpretation, often they are uncertain whether or not the process followed in a direct interpretation can simply be applied to the intermediary interpreting process. Findings noted in this research, however, clearly indicate that the process is quite different. Techniques used in direct interpretations are altered when functioning in the intermediary role, and other additional strategies may need to be employed. Increasing pause and pause/hold times, direct eye gaze, head nods, fingerspelling concepts without expansions, and other techniques noted in this study offer some concrete suggestions for how direct interpretations can be altered in intermediary interpreting settings. Interpreters functioning in the intermediary role can apply the techniques described in this study as they begin to shape their interpretations to meet the demands inherent in this process. The discoveries observed in this research serve only as a starting point for future discussions and explorations into this complex task.

Evidence generated in the analysis of the data in this research indicates a clear distinction between how interpreters function in intermediary as opposed to direct interpretation settings. Although some of these distinctions were observed and documented, they do not represent the entire range of differences that exist. Assuredly, data collected from other Deaf/hearing teams would reveal additional alterations that have been made by the hearing interpreter when functioning in this role. Future research that includes more Deaf/hearing interpreting teams is necessary. Findings from these studies may help to distinguish team-specific alterations as opposed to alterations observed across the board. These types of studies can help to establish the validity and reliability of the findings observed in data collected for this research. Once observable patterns across other Deaf/hearing teams are documented, greater generalizability of results can be suggested.

Studies of specific aspects of the intermediary interpretation can be undertaken to document other techniques specific to the intermediary interpreting process. For example, one specific area of recommended future study relates to decisions about the intermediary target language. Does the hearing interpreter follow a more English-based word order when in this role? How do the Deaf interpreter's bi-lingual skills impact the decision to use English or ASL syntax? Is the intermediary interpreter functioning more as an intermediary transliterator by producing more English grammatical structures? These questions as well as others related to the target language deserve more investigation.

Additional research related to the interpersonal and intercultural relationship formed between the Deaf and hearing interpreter would be insightful as well. How do issues of oppression affect this working relationship? What relational issues, such as trust, are inherent to a successful, well-functioning team? What kind of dialogue should take place between the two interpreters prior to the start of the task?

The stimulus material selected for the interpretation in this study was nearly culturally neutral. The hearing speaker did not use any culture-specific terms, or phrases, nor were any references made that could be considered culturally bound. It would be interesting to analyze data collected in a similar experiment where the source message contained specific references to cultures other than the Deaf culture. Hearing interpreters have typically been responsible to facilitate the understanding of this type of information across cultural boundaries. Analysis of data in a setting such as this may reveal the extent to which the hearing interpreter relies on the Deaf interpreter to function as a cultural mediator instead of performing this task themselves. Future research in this area is also necessary.

Well beyond the scope of this research are other questions related to the overall effectiveness of Deaf/hearing relay teams. One often stated concern is that of message equivalence and accuracy. Once the source message is channeled through not one, but two interpretations, how close is the target message to the intended source? Future studies may also be directed at audience satisfaction levels. Are Deaf consumers able to better understand a message from a Deaf/hearing team than from an interpreter working independently? Are message comprehension levels higher when more native-like, cultural interpretations are delivered?

The findings of this research only begin to uncover some of the unique characteristics of intermediary interpretations. Much more research in this area is necessary to better understand how interpreters function as members of a relay team. The results and suggestions offered in this study are only catalysts aimed at initiating future dialogue and scholarly research on this topic.

Conclusions

Although research indicates a desire by Deaf audience members for interpretations in ASL to occur, non-native, hearing interpreters often produce a target message that contains much of the form of the English language. The introduction of native ASL Deaf relay interpreters into the interpreting process, would seem to rectify this dilemma. However, due to the lack of research in this area, Deaf/hearing relay teams are not being hired in many instances. The goal of this research study was to determine if there are physically observable differences between a direct interpretation, where the hearing interpreter is working directly from the source into the target language, and an intermediary interpretation, where the source message is "fed" to a Deaf interpreter. Differences were observed in six areas: 1) pausing, 2) eye gaze, 3) head nods, 4) the number of signs produced per minute, 5) fingerspelling versus signs, and 6) clarifications between the two interpreters.

In the comparison of the two interpretations, an increased pause time with or without hold was observed to have occurred in the intermediary interpretation. Unlike in the direct interpretation, where the interpreter's eyes were typically gazing downward during these pauses, in the intermediary interpretation, the interpreter's eyes were directed at the Deaf interpreter. The focused eye gaze accompanied with an increase in monitoring head nods indicate an intentional effort on the part of the hearing interpreter to regulate the Deaf interpreter's source message intake and target message output.

Analysis of the two interpretations also revealed that the interpreter in the intermediary position used 24 less signs per minute than were used in the direct interpretation. One way the interpreter was able to reduce the number of signs produced per minute and yet continue to strive for message equivalency was by fingerspelling particular signs and concepts rather than utilizing expansion techniques. The expansion of the concept then became the responsibility of the Deaf interpreter.

Finally, dialogues between the two interpreters for clarification purposes were observed to have occurred several times during the intermediary interpretation. It was during these instances that mis-fed information was corrected and requests for repetition were made. Both the Deaf and hearing interpreters initiated these clarification dialogues.

Clearly, the question of whether or not differences exist

between a direct interpretation and an intermediary interpretation has been answered. The results of this research have shed some light on how the two processes differ from one another. These findings offer baseline data that can be used in the training of Deaf/hearing relay teams. It is hoped that this research as well as any future research that follows in this area will provide the training tools necessary to increase the pool of qualified Deaf/hearing relay teams.

Appendix A - Example Transcription of Direct Interpretation

Entry No	Sentence Gloss	Right hand Gloss	Left hand Gloss	Eye Gaze	Pause Hold	Pause
				aud = audience		
				d=down		
				rt=right		
				lf=down		
				u = up		
				mid = middle		
				cl = classifier		
1		NOW				
2		IX	IX	mid		
3		NEW		mid		
4	NOW IX NEW #CAR	#CAR		rt/up	0.96	
5		#CO	IX	rt/up		
6		PRO		rt/up		
7		NEW		rt/up		
8	#CO PRO NEW #CAR	#CAR	elbow point	rt/up		
9		sf		rt/up		
10		HAVE		aud		
11		CL: belt		aud		
12		ADD		aud		
13		PRO		up		
14		#COMPANY		up		
15		START		aud		
16		NOW		aud		
17		ADD		aud		
18	HAVE CL: belt ADD PRO #CO START NOW ADD CL: BELT	CL: belt	touch lf shoulder	d		
19		itches cheek	WAIT-A-MINUTE	d	1.30	
20		PRO		aud		
21		SAY		aud		
22		IMPORTANT		aud		
23		FOR		mid		
24	PRO SAY IMPORTANT FOR CHILDREN	CHILDREN		aud		
25		BACK		rt		
26		ALL(?)		aud		
27		CHILDREN		aud		
28		SIT		aud		
29		BACK		aud		
30		RIGHT		aud		
31		MEAN		d		
32		CHILDREN		d		
33		CL: waist belt	lf waist	d		
34		ONLY-ONE		d		
35	BACK ALL(?) CHILDREN SIT BACK RIGHT MEAN CHILDREN CL: waist belt ONLY-ONE SILLY!	SILLY!		aud		
36		ADD		aud		
37		CL: belt	touch lf shoulder	d		
38		GOOD		d		
39	ADD CL: belt GOOD gesture: "a_ok"	gesture: "a-ok"		d		
40	rest	rests		d		0.9
41		PRO-lf		rt		
42		NOW++++		d		
43		STILL		aud		
44		LEAVE+ (bs?)		d		
45		OLD		d		
46		#CAR	elbow point	d		
47		NONE		aud		
48		CL: belt	touch lf shoulder	aud		
49		BACK		d		
50		MEAN		d		
51		TOTAL-OF		d		
52		1		d		
53		HUNDRED		d		
54		FORTY		d		
55		THOUSAND		aud		
56		CAR		d		
57		LEFT		d		
58		STILL		d		

#						
59		NONE		aud		
60	PRO-II NOW++++ STILL LEAVE+ OLD #CAR NONE CL: belt BACK MEAN TOTAL-OF 1 HUNDRED FORTY THOUSAND CAR LEFT STILL NONE CL: belt	CL: belt	touch lf shoulder	aud		
61		STILL		d		
62		USE+		aud		
63	STILL USE+ EVERYDAY	EVERYDAY		aud		
64		rests		d		2.07
65		nms: topic?		d		
66		PRO		d		
67		#CAR		d		
69	PRO #CAR NOW NEW	NEW		d		
70		SINCE		d		
71		19		up/rt		
72		80		up/rt		
73		19		up/rt		
74		90	(left)	up/rt		
75	SINCE 19 80 19 90 PRO-rt	PRO-rt		d		

Journal of Interpretation

Appendix B - Example Transcription Of Intermediary Interpretation

Entry No.	Sentence Gloss	Right hand Gloss	Left hand Gloss	Eye Gaze	Pause Hold	Pause
				aud = audience		
				d=down		
				rt=right		
				lf=down		
				u = up		
				mid = middle		
				cl = classifier		
1		hn		aud		
2		NOW		d		
3		RECENTLY		rt		
4		BACK		rt		
5		HAVE		aud		
6	NOW RECENTLY BACK HAVE CL: BELT	CL: BELT		aud	3.30	
7		hn		aud		
8		hn		aud		
9		hn		aud		
10		hn		aud		
11		IMPORTANT		aud		
12		sf		aud		
13		SPECIAL		aud		
14		FOR		aud		
15	IMPORTANT SPECIAL FOR CHILDREN	CHILDREN		aud		
16		I-F		aud		
17		PRO		rt		
18		HAVE		rt		
19		FAMILY		rt		
20		HAVE		rt		
21	I-F PRO HAVE FAMILY HAVE CHILDREN	CHILDREN		more rt		
22		MEAN		rt		
23		CL: seated	CL: seated	rt		
24	MEAN CL: seated BACK	BACK		rt		
25		CHILDREN		aud		
26		WHO		aud		
27		CHILDREN		aud		
28	CHILDREN WHO CHILDREN BACK	BACK		aud		
29		MEAN		d		

30		CL: belt	shoulder-lf	aud		
31	MEAN CL: belt IMPORTANT	IMPORTANT		emphasis		
32		rests		d/aud		2.60
33		STILL		aud		
34		NOW+		rt		
35		CAR		rt up		
36		HOW-MANY		u		
37		TOTAL		u		
38		#CAR		u		
39		NOW		aud		
40	STILL NOW+ CAR HOW-MANY TOTAL #CAR NOW STILL	STILL		aud		
41		ONE		aud		
42		HUNDRED	touch elbow	aud		
43		FORTY		aud		
44		MILLION		aud		
45		NONE		aud		
46	ONE HUNDRED FORTY MILLION NONE CL: belt	CL: belt	lf shoulder	aud	2.51	
47		rests		aud/d		3.77
48		NOW+		d		
49		#CAR	IX	d		
50	NOW #CAR SINCE	SINCE		d		
51		fs: late		d		
52		19		d		
53		80		d		
54		S		d		
55		TO		d		
56		19		d		
57		90		d		
58	L-A-T-E 19 80 S TO 19 90 S	S		aud	2.13	
59		FRONT++		aud		
60		HAVE		aud		
61		sf		aud		
62		fs: automatic	IX elbow	aud		
63		fs: restraints		aud		
64	FRONT++ HAVE fs: automatic fs: restraints	fs: restraints		aud		
65		rests		aud		5.51
66		PROBLEM		d		
67	PROBLEM DIFFERENT+++	DIFFERENT+++		d		
68		SOME		d		
69		WOW	WOW	d		
70		TRUE	IX	d		
71	SOME WOW TRUE AWFUL	AWFUL		d		

References

Baker, C., & Cokely, D. (1980). *American sign language: A teacher's resource text on grammar and culture.* Silver Spring, MD: T. J. Publishers.

Baker-Shenk, C. (1986). Characteristics of oppressed and oppressor peoples: Their effect on the interpreting context. In M. McIntire (Ed.), *Interpreting: The art of cross cultural mediation. Proceedings of the Ninth National Convention of the Registry of Interpreters for the Deaf* (pp. 43-54). Silver Spring, MD: RID Publications.

Cokely, D. (1992). *Interpretation: A sociolinguistic model.* Burtonsville, MD: Linstock Press.

Fleischer, L. (1975). *Sign language interpretation under four interpreting conditions.* Unpublished doctoral dissertation, Brigham Young University, Salt Lake City, Utah. (University microfilm).

Fleischer, L., & M. Cottrell (1976). Sign language interpretation under four interpreting conditions. In H.J. Murphy (Ed.), *Selected readings in the integration of deaf students at CSUN.* (Center on Deafness Publication Series No. 1). Northridge, CA: California State University.

Frishberg, N. (1990). *Interpreting: An introduction.* Silver Spring, MD: RID Publications.

Kendon, A. (1967). Some functions of gaze-direction in social interaction. *Acta Psychologica 26,* 32-49.

Livingston, S., Singer, B. and Abrahamson, T. (1994). Effectiveness compared: ASL interpretation vs.transliteration. *Sign Language Studies, 82,* 1-54.

Llewellyn-Jones, P. (1981). Simultaneous interpreting. In *Perspectives on British Sign Language and deafness.* London: Croom Helm Ltd.

Murphy, H., & Fleischer, L. (1977). The effects of Ameslan versus Siglish upon test scores. *Journal of Rehabilitation of the Deaf, 2,* 15-18.

Nida, E. & C. Taber (1974). *The theory and practice of translation.* Leiden: E.J. Brill.

Winston, E. (1990). Techniques for improving accent in sign language interpreters. In A. Wilson (Ed.), *Looking Ahead: Proceedings of the 31st Annual Conference of the American Translators Association.* (pp. 47-57). Medford, NJ: Learned Information Inc.

Zimmer, J. (1989). ASL/English interpreting in an interactive setting. In D. Lindberg-Hammond (Ed.), *Proceedings of the 30th Annual Conference of the American Translators Association* (pp. 225-231). Medford, NJ: Learned Information, Inc.

Journal of Interpretation

A Study of the Demographics of Attendees at the 1997 Biennial Convention of the Registry of Interpreters for the Deaf, Inc.

Linda K. Stauffer, M.Ed., CSC
Assistant Professor, Interpreter Training Program
University of Arkansas at Little Rock

Daniel D. Burch, Ph.D., CSC
President, Registry of Interpreters for the Deaf, Inc.

Steven E. Boone, Ph.D.
Director of Research
University of Arkansas RRTC
for Persons who are Deaf or Hard of Hearing

A Study of the Demographics of Attendees at the 1997 Biennial Convention of the Registry of Interpreters for the Deaf, Inc.

Linda K. Stauffer, M.Ed., CSC
Assistant Professor, Interpreter Training Program
University of Arkansas at Little Rock

Daniel D. Burch, P.h.D., CSC
President, Registry of Interpreters for the Deaf, Inc.

Steven E. Boone, Ph.D.
Director of Research
University of Arkansas RRTC
for Persons Who Are Deaf or Hard of Hearing

Abstract

There is a national crisis in the quality, quantity, and qualifications of sign language interpreters (National Association for the Deaf-Registry of Interpreters for the Deaf [NAD-RID], 1994). However, literature describing the number and demographic profile of the interpreter workforce is limited. Neither of these organizations has current demographic information regarding their membership, and the last major study of all interpreters was reported almost 20 years ago (Cokely, 1981). Responding to this need, this study presents demographic characteristics of a sample of interpreters attending the 1997 Biennial Conference of the Registry of Interpreters for the Deaf. Recommendations are proposed to establish an ongoing demographic database of interpreters who are members of RID as well as to conduct a national survey of all interpreters, including those certified by other entities.

Introduction

There is a national crisis in the quality, quantity, and qualifications of sign language interpreters (National Association for the Deaf-Registry of Interpreters for the Deaf [NAD-RID], 1994). The best estimate of the number of sign language interpreters in the United States is 25,000 based upon affiliation with RID (Burch, 1998). The actual number and demographic characteristics of the interpreting workforce, including these individuals and others, are largely a matter of conjecture. Studies that describe the population of interpreters of American Sign Language and English are conspicuous by their absence in the literature. The singular study thus far reported was conducted almost 20 years ago (Cokely, 1981).

Two organizations certify interpreters at the national level. The Registry of Interpreters for the Deaf (RID) is the oldest and largest association of interpreters of American Sign Language and English in the United States (Burch, 1996; Caccamise et al., 1980; Frishberg, 1990; Stewart, Schein, & Cartwright, 1998; Quigley & Youngs, 1965). RID reports a certified workforce of over 3,000 individuals (D. Stebbins, personal communication, 1998). The National Association of the Deaf (NAD) is the oldest and largest deafness-related consumer organization in the United States and has recently embarked on a certification process of its own. NAD reports a certified workforce of approximately 1,500 divided across five levels of skill (N. Rarus, personal communication, 1997).

Descriptive information regarding the characteristics of interpreters from either of these organizations is limited. RID does not currently collect or maintain general demographic information in its membership database (C.Nettles, personal communication, 1998). The last available data regarding these interpreters was collected in the early 1990s and never reported. Similarly, NAD does not collect demographic information on its certified interpreters (P. Annarino, personal communication, 1998). Even less is known about the over 20,000 interpreters who are not certified or affiliated with either organization.

This study was initiated in order to help meet this need for descriptive information. Interpreters that were attending the 1997 Biennial Convention of RID were asked to respond to a brief questionnaire regarding their demographic characteristics, training, and qualifications. While not representative of all interpreters in the workforce, the Convention provided cost-effective access to a potential sample of over 1,000 interpreters from across the United States.

Purpose of the Study

The primary purpose of this study was to collect a snapshot of the characteristics of practitioners of the profession of interpreting American Sign Language and English who are members of RID and who attend national conventions. The study was specifically designed to investigate the following questions:

- What is the gender profile of the interpreting community?
- What is the age profile of the interpreting workforce?
- What is the ethnic profile of the interpreting workforce?
- What certification levels do respondents represent?
- What degrees have been attained by interpreters in what fields of study?
- How did interpreters learn sign language?
- How did interpreters learn to interpret?

Data on similar questions regarding the membership of RID, based upon the information last collected in the early 1990s, is also presented. While not directly comparable, this information does provide a context in which to look at changes in the interpreting profession.

Method

Subjects
Subjects were participants at the 1997 Biennial Convention of RID. Held in Long Beach, California, the conference was attended by approximately 1,000 interpreters. A total of 201 interpreters voluntarily completed the research questionnaire that was placed in the registration packet.

Instrument
A written questionnaire was developed for this study. The survey requested general demographic information (e.g., gender, age, ethnic background, certification, and degree/s attained, and how sign language and interpreting were learned). Ethnic categories were adopted from the National

Multicultural Interpreting Project classifications (M. Mooney, personal correspondence, 1998). Face and content validity of the instrument was documented via review by the RID Board of Directors.

RID Membership Data

Descriptive information was obtained from RID regarding the last available demographics of the RID membership. This information, collected in 1990-91 and 1991-92, was based upon 3,070 and 2,232 persons, respectively. Data was hand tabulated, but never reported (S. Sullivan, personal communication, 1996).

Procedures

The study was conducted with the approval of the RID Board of Directors. Questionnaires were placed in the convention registration packets of all attendees. Respondents were asked to voluntarily complete and return the questionnaire to the "Help Hut" (a central information location at each Biennial Convention). The resulting data was entered and analyzed using SPSS/PC+ statistical modules. These analyses were conducted with technical assistance from the University of Arkansas Rehabilitation Research and Training Center for Persons Who Are Deaf or Hard of Hearing.

Results and Discussion

Of the total 1,013 individuals registered for the 1997 Biennial Convention, 201 individuals completed the survey inserted into the registration packet. This constitutes a return rate of 19.8%. This return rate was consistent with similar descriptive studies conducted at conventions of other organizations.

Table 1 provides frequency and percentage rates by gender. Respondents were primarily female (79%). As may be seen in the table, this finding is consistent with prior data regarding RID membership collected in the early 1990s. This consistency indicates that the profession remains heavily dominated by females.

Tables 2 and 3 represent the age distribution of 1997 Convention respondents. As may be seen in the Table, the majority of the respondents (nearly 72%) range from their 30s to 40s. This finding is consistent with prior membership data collected in 1991 and 1992. Interestingly, the percentage of younger individuals responding remains low, with less than 15% under age 29. If this finding continues, the field will experience further major shortages, over and above the current shortage, by the year 2,010 when the youngest of those age ranges begins to reach retirement age.

Table 1
Gender Distribution

Gender	1997 Convention		1991-92		1990-91	
	f	%	f	%	f	%
Female	158	78.6	2,636	85.9	1,999	86.1
Male	43	21.4	426	13.9	324	13.9
No Response	0	0.0	8	0.3	613	26.4
Totals	201	100.0	3,070	100.0	2,323	100.0

Table 2
1997 Convention Age Distribution

Age Range	1997 Convention	
	f	%
18-29	29	14.4
30-39	74	36.8
40-49	70	34.8
50-59	18	9.0
60+	8	4.0
No Response	2	1.0
Totals	201	100.0

Table 3
Previous Survey Age Distribution

Age Range	1991-92		1990-91	
	f	%	f	%
< 18	0	0.0	116	3.9
18-25	184	6.0	1,401	47.7
26-39	1,841	60.5	656	22.3
40-55	862	28.3	143	4.9
55+	158	5.2	622	21.2
Totals	3,045	100.0	2,938	100.0

Table 4 indicates the ethnic profile of the respondents and prior membership surveys. As may be seen in the Table, interpreters are overwhelmingly (80%) European, a finding that is consistent with prior membership studies. Of note is that the percentage of respondents from diverse racial-ethnic groups has increased from 5% in 1990-91, 7.5% in 1991-92, to 8% in the 1997 Convention. While a promising trend, there appears to be an ongoing need to attract members of diverse groups into the profession.

Table 4
Ethnic Distribution

Ethnicity	Convention 1997		1991-92		1990-91	
	f	%	f	%	f	%
African/Black	4	2.0	61	2.2	34	1.2
Asian	2	1.0	22	0.8	18	0.6
European	161	80.1	2,454	89.4	2,123	72.3
Hispanic/Latino	5	2.5	47	1.7	39	1.3
Native American	6	3.0	77	2.8	55	1.9
Other	0	0.0	43	1.6	28	1.0
No Response	23	11.4	40	1.5	641	21.8
Totals	201	100.0	2,744	100.0	2,938	100.0

Table 5 indicates the certificates that 1997 Convention Survey respondents held. Of the interpreters responding, the most common certificate tends to be interpreting (46 individuals attained a Certificate of Interpretation). The second most common certificate tends to be transliterating (36 attained their Certificate of Transliteration, and 21 attained a Transliteration Certificate). Nearly 20% (41 of 201) carried no certification. The vast majority (80%) had at least one certificate, and nearly half (43%) had a second certificate. The numbers greatly diminish at the level of three certificates or more (6.6% had three or more certificates).

Table 6 indicates the level of the degrees attained by respondents and members. Nearly 85% of the 1997 Convention respondents reported having a college degree. When compared to prior membership data, the percentages of interpreters with degrees appears to be increasing: 58% during 1990-91 and 73% during 1991-92. Also of note is the specific degree held. Over 15% of the respondents had degrees in interpreting. This finding represents a substantial increase when compared with earlier membership surveys (3.6% in 1990-91).

Table 5
Distribution of Certificates

Certification	f	%
CI	60	18.1
CT	67	20.2
CSC	46	13.9
IC	24	7.3
TC	25	7.6
RSC	7	2.1
CDI-P	1	0.3
OIC:C	6	1.8
OIC:S/V	3	0.9
OIC:V/S	0	0
OTC	1	0.3
SC:L	6	1.8
SC:L Prov	1	0.3
CLIP	3	0.9
Candidate	7	2.1
NAD III	6	1.8
NAD IV	6	1.8
NAD V	4	1.2
State	5	1.5
QA	7	2.1
None	41	12.4
Other	5	1.5
Totals	331	99.9[*]

* Total does not equal 100 percent due to rounding error

Table 7 indicates in what major areas degrees were attained. Degree emphasis at the associates level was in interpreting (62%). At the bachelors level, degree emphasis remained with interpreting (15%), but also includes the areas of psychology (10%) and deaf education (8%). At the masters level, deaf education and counseling (each at 15%) were the degree emphases. No clear percentage was evident at the doctoral level, as there were only four respondents with four different degrees.

Table 8 indicates where respondents learned sign language.

Approximately half (50%) of the respondents to the 1997 Convention Survey learned signs through Interpreter Preparation Programs (27%) and workshops/classes (23%). Learning through friends (25%) was also a major source of sign language learning. Although data are not available to support it, interpreters in the past were generally known to have been predominantly children of deaf adults (CODAs) or workers in the churches. These two training grounds appear to have been supplanted by formal courses of study in colleges and universities.

Similarly, the method of learning to interpret has also shifted from informal methods to more formal training programs. Table 9 shows that respondents to the 1997 Convention Survey indicated the predominant method of learning to interpret was formal training (65%) in Interpreter Preparation Programs (39%) and workshops/classes (26%). Learning to interpret from friends was also indicated as a major way of learning to interpret (16%). As with learning to sign, learning to interpret has apparently moved from the community into formal preparation programs.

Table 6
Distribution of Degrees

Degree	Convention 1997		1991-92		1990-91	
	f	%	f	%	f	%
HS	4	2.0	237	7.8	181	6.2
Some College/						
IPP Cert.	29	14.4		0.0		0.0
AA/AS	40	19.9	492	16.1	371	12.6
BA/BS	72	35.8	914	30.0	710	24.2
MA/MS	36	17.9	739	24.2	570	19.4
MA+ 30	17	8.5		0.0		0.0
PhD/EdD	3	1.5	82	2.7	70	2.4
No Response	0	0.0	584	19.2	1,036	35.3
Totals	201	100.0	3,048	100.0	2,938	100.0

Table 7
Distribution of Degree Majors

	Associate		Bachelor		Master		Doctorate	
	f	%	f	%	f	%	f	%
ASL/Deaf Studies	4	8.9	5	6.8		0.0		0.0
Business	2	4.4	2	2.7	1	1.8		0.0
Communications/Media		0.0	5	6.8	3	5.5		0.0
Counseling		0.0		0.0	8	14.5		0.0
Education	3	6.7	2	2.7	5	9.1		0.0
Education of the Deaf		0.0	6	8.2	8	14.5		0.0
Educational Interpreting	2	4.4	1	1.4		0.0		0.0
English		0.0	4	5.5		0.0		0.0
Interpreting	28	62.2	11	15.1	2	3.6		0.0
Law	1	2.2	1	1.4		0.0		0.0
Liberal Arts	4	8.9	3	4.1	1	1.8		0.0
Linguistics		0.0	1	1.4	2	3.6	1	25.0
Medical	1	2.2		0.0		0.0		0.0
Philosophy		0.0	1	1.4		0.0		0.0
Political Science		0.0	1	1.4		0.0		0.0
Psychology		0.0	7	9.6	5	9.1	1	25.0
Religion		0.0	2	2.7		0.0		0.0
Science		0.0	4	5.5	4	7.3		0.0
Social Work		0.0	2	2.7	3	5.5		0.0
Sociology		0.0	4	5.5	2	3.6		0.0
Special Education		0.0		0.0	2	3.6	1	25.0
Speech Pathology		0.0	4	5.5	4	7.3		0.0
Teaching Interpreting		0.0		0.0	2	3.6		0.0
Theater		0.0	4	5.5	3	5.5		0.0
Other		0.0	3	4.1			1	25.0
Totals	45	100.0	73	100.0	55	100.0	4	100.0

Table 8
Sign Language Training Distribution

Learned Signs*	*f*	%
Parents	32	8.4
Children	2	0.5
Church	17	4.5
ITP	102	26.9
Siblings	7	1.8
Friends	94	24.8
Workshops/Classes	86	22.7
Work	4	1.1
Self	6	1.6
Other	29	7.7
Totals	379	100.0

* Multiple Responses

Table 9
Interpreter Training Distribution

Learned Interpreting*	*f*	%
Parents	23	6.8
Children	2	0.6
Church	20	5.9
ITP	131	38.9
Siblings	4	1.2
Friends	54	16.0
Workshops/Classes	89	26.4
Work	11	3.3
Self	3	0.9
Totals	337	100.0

* Multiple Responses

Conclusions, Limitations, and Recommendations

Conclusions

This study has presented a timely snapshot of the demographic characteristics of interpreters who attended and responded to a survey at the 1997 Convention. Much of this snapshot is highly consistent with previous data that was collected in the early 90s. Several trends were noted when comparing this sample with prior data. However, it is necessary to view these trends with caution given differences in the questionnaire used, sampling techniques (attendees versus membership), and the number of individuals who responded. These findings may not be representative of the total membership of RID, let alone the total workforce of interpreters.

A number of positive trends were found. The sample was slightly more diverse and included a slight increase in the number of male respondents. Aging of the respondents, similar to the general population of workers, points to the need to attract more persons into the field. Interestingly, it appears that the sample had benefitted from more formal training in sign language and interpreting. Survey data indicate that convention attendees tend to be certified and had degrees. This finding is in contrast to the general view that the profession is predominantly non-degreed (Professional Development Committee, personal communication, 1998).

Recommendations

There are obvious benefits to be gained from collecting demographic data to validate these findings and to clarify some of the trends. This information would be useful in documenting shortages of interpreters and their training needs. Toward this goal, it is recommended that RID re-institute the practice of collecting demographic data as part of its membership renewal campaign. Data collected should be comprehensive, including demographic characteristics, credentials, and training. By collecting this information on an annual basis, a true longitudinal study could be designed to validate trends alluded to in this study.

Finally, it is recommended that a national survey be conducted to address similar issues with all interpreters, not just those who choose to affiliate with and are certified by RID. Given the obvious benefits of having a complete picture of the workforce, it is recommended that RID advocate to public and private funding agencies to obtain support for this study.

References

Burch, D. D. (1996). *RID record* (2nd ed.). Silver Spring, MD: Registry of Interpreters for the Deaf Publications.

Burch, D. D. (1998, May, July, October). *RID into the 21st century: The power of our collective wisdom in action.* Paper presented at the meetings of the Region Conferences of the Registry of Interpreters for the Deaf, Phoenix, AZ; Ft. Lauderdale, FL; Chicago, IL; Little Rock, AR; Rochester, NY.

Caccamise, F., Dirst, R., DeVries, R.D., Heil, J., Kirchner, C., Kirchner, S., Rinaldi, A.M., & Stangarone, J. (1980). *Introduction to interpreting for interpreters/transliterators, hearing impaired consumers & hearing consumers.* Silver Spring, MD: Registry of Interpreters for the Deaf Publications.

Cokely, D. (1981). Sign Language interpreters: A demographic survey. *Sign Language Studies, 32,* 261-286.

Frishberg, N. (1990). *Interpreting: An introduction* (Rev. ed.). Silver Spring, MD: Registry of Interpreters for the Deaf Publications.

National Association of the Deaf-Registry of Interpreters for the Deaf. (March, 1994). National interpreter crisis declared. *Registry of Interpreters for the Deaf (RID) VIEWS, 11,* 1, 6.

Stewart, D. A., Schein, J. D., & Cartwright, B. E. (1998). *Sign language interpreting: Exploring its art and science.* Boston, MA: Allyn and Bacon.

Quigley, S. P., & Youngs, J. (Eds.) (1965). *Interpreting for deaf people.* Washington, D.C.: United States Department of Health, Education and Welfare, Vocational Rehabilitation Administration.

Journal of Interpretation

The Professionalization
of Community Interpreting

Holly Mikkelson
Monterey Institute of International Studies

Reprinted with permission. *The ATA Chronicle*, March 1998.

The Professionalization
of Community Interpreting

Holly Mikkelson
Monterey Institute of International Studies

Reprinted with permission. The ATA Chronicle, March 1998.

Abstract

Community interpreting, which includes court and medical interpreting, is following the typical pattern of a profession in its infancy. In the beginning it is characterized by a lack of standards for training and practice, disorganization and disunity among practitioners, a lack of recognition of the profession among clients and the public, and poor working conditions. These circumstances improve as practitioners unite and form professional associations to impose discipline and standardization and to achieve recognition through education, legislation, and public relations. This paper will define the terms "community interpreting" and "profession," present a comparative analysis of community interpreting and other professions, and recommend a course of action to promote the profession in the medium and long terms.

Definition of Terms

Community Interpreting

Community interpreting has been defined in a variety of ways, ranging from the kind of interpreting that takes place informally in neighborhoods and community agencies, and is performed by amateurs or ad hoc interpreters (Ref. 1, p. 29), to a more formal occupation involving practitioners with some training in medical, legal, or social service interpreting (Ref. 2). Roda Roberts (Ref. 3) provides a more detailed discussion of these definitions. This paper employs the definition found in the announcement of the First International Conference on Interpreting in Legal, Health and Social Service Settings:

> Community Interpreting enables people who are not fluent speakers of the official language(s) of the country to communicate with the providers of pub-

lic services so as to facilitate full and equal access to legal, health, education, government, and social services (Ref. 4).

Thus, community interpreting is distinguished from other types of interpreting, such as conference or escort interpreting, in that the services are provided to the residents of the community in which the interpreting takes place, not to conference delegates, diplomats, or professionals traveling abroad to conduct business. Other distinctions that set community interpreting apart from conference interpreting are identified by Roberts (Ref. 3): 1) Community interpreters primarily serve to ensure access to public services, and are therefore likely to work in institutional settings; 2) they are more apt to be interpreting dialogue-like interactions than speeches; 3) they routinely interpret into and out of both or all of their working languages; 4) the presence of the community interpreter is much more noticeable in the communication process than is that of the conference interpreter; 5) a great many languages, many of them minority languages that are not the language of government in any country, are interpreted at the community level, unlike the limited number of languages of international diplomacy and commerce handled by conference and escort interpreters; and 6) community interpreters are often viewed as advocates or "cultural brokers" who go beyond the traditional neutral role of the interpreter.

Other terms have been used to describe this activity. In the United Kingdom, for example, "public service interpreting" is the preferred term; while in Canada, "cultural interpreting" is often used. Other designations include "dialogue interpreting" and "ad hoc interpreting." "Community interpreting" seems to be the term most widely accepted in the literature, however (Ref. 3).

Profession

The American Heritage Dictionary of the English Language defines the term "profession" as "1) an occupation or vocation requiring training in the liberal arts or the sciences and advanced study in a specialized field; 2) the body of qualified persons of one specific occupation or field." The term has been used in a variety of contexts throughout history, beginning with the religious connotation of taking vows or expressing a belief. The sense of an occupation or calling came along later.

In modern times, medicine, law, and the ministry have been considered the original "learned professions" (jokes about the "first profession" notwithstanding), and are regarded as models for others to emulate (Ref. 5, p. 13). This is especially true of medicine, which has reached the pinnacle of prestige and power in the United States. Sociologists, in particular, have studied the process whereby an occupation becomes a profession and thus enhances the social status of its practitioners.

This discussion of professionalization centers on the work of Joseph Tseng (Ref. 5), who has written a comprehensive review of the literature on professionalism and developed his own model based on conference interpreting in Taiwan. After presenting Tseng's findings and conclusions, I will apply his model to community interpreting in the United States.

Professionalization

Tseng reviews the writings of a number of scholars who have examined the process whereby an occupation becomes a profession. He identifies two schools of thought, those who accept the "trait theory" of professionalization and those who uphold the "theory of control."

Trait Theory

The trait theory states that an occupation becomes a profession by attaining certain characteristics, including adherence to a code of ethics, a body of theoretical knowledge, licensure or registration, and loyalty to colleagues. Proponents of the trait theory have devised checklists of attributes that can be ticked off to determine how far a given occupation has progressed toward the goal of professionalization (Ref. 6).

Theory of Control

The theory of control, on the other hand, goes beyond internal characteristics and looks at how the occupation relates to other components of the labor market and institutions in society. According to this view, the more control practitioners of an occupation are able to exert over the substance of their work and the market in which they operate, the more professionalized the occupation. Tseng notes that the theory of control views professions in terms of the amount of power they wield, and that professionalization is a collective effort rather than an individual one: "Powerful professions are characterized by powerful associations" (Ref. 5, p. 20). An occupational group can exert both internal control (over the body of knowledge and training required for entry into the field and the behavior or ethics of the practitioners) and external control (working conditions and relations with clients). The legal profession, for example, defines not only the curriculum of law schools and the content of bar exams, but also the standards for training and testing in related occupations (paralegals, court reporters, court clerks). As a result, these related occupations have comparatively little autonomy and are less likely to attain the degree of professionalization that lawyers and judges enjoy.

One element of prestigious professions that has often been remarked upon is the mystification of the specialized knowledge acquired by practitioners. Often the aura of mystique is created by using terms of art and jargon when "talking shop" with colleagues, thus excluding the uninitiated from the dialogue (Ref. 7, pp. 40-41). A profession that succeeds in mystifying its expertise is able to control the market by prohibiting interlopers from practicing the profession.

A corollary to the mystification principle is the notion that professions gain power by defining the needs of their clients rather than allowing the clients to set the agenda (Ref. 8). Thus, until recently it was virtually impossible to obtain a divorce without retaining an attorney, because it was impossible for a layperson to know what he needed to do to achieve the goal of legally severing marital bonds. It was not until a few reformers wrested that power away from attorneys by writing self-help books, complete with sample forms and detailed checklists, that it finally became possible to accomplish an uncontested divorce without retained counsel. (If any property or children are involved in the divorce, which is usually the case, it is still impossible to proceed without a lawyer.) If a client is able to come to a practitioner and say, "I know what I want, just help me with the technicalities," as in the case of an interior decorator or a hairdresser, the occupation does not have a great deal of autonomy or power. If the client is able to understand what the practitioner is doing to help him accomplish his goal, he maintains a certain amount of control over the transaction. On the other hand, if he consults a physician who performs a strange test on a mysterious machine, for example, he has no means of challenging or questioning the physician's judgment.

The theory of control also posits that powerful professions establish alliances with the state. If they are perceived as performing a service that benefits the public, the state will grant them special privileges and independence. They are more likely to be self-regulated than other occupations (consider the Bar Association's role in writing bar exam and disciplining its members, for example), and this autonomy, in turn, enhances the public's trust in the profession (Ref. 9).

Tseng concludes that the theory of control is more useful than the trait theory for understanding how an occupation becomes a profession, but it fails to provide guidelines for an occupation that aspires to achieve that objective. Consequently, he provides his own model of professionalization, which draws upon elements of trait and control theory and adds components based on his experience with conference interpreting.

Tseng Model

According to Tseng, the first phase in the process of professionalization is market disorder. This period is characterized by fierce competition among the practitioners of an occupation:

> Practitioners in the market cannot keep outsiders from entering practice. They themselves may have started practice as outsiders or quacks. Recipients of the service either have very little understanding of what practitioners do or very little confidence in the services they receive. It is very likely that the public simply does not care about the quality of the services. Hence, distrust and misunderstanding permeate the market. What matters more to clients, in the absence of quality control, is usually price. Whoever demands the lowest fees gets the job. ... When the clients need services, they simply call upon anyone who is around and asking a reasonable fee. Clients who demand quality services are usually troubled by the fact that they do not know where to get qualified practitioners for services (Ref. 5, pp. 44-45).

Unlike doctors or lawyers, who are able to mystify their occupations, interpreters deal with clients who *think* they know what interpreters do (and think it is very simple), but in fact do not. Furthermore, in many cases (especially in community interpreting settings) the professionals who work with interpreters do not value the interpreting service nearly as much as a patient values his health or a legal client his freedom. The upshot is that interpreting is not mystified by the client's ignorance, but merely devalued.

In such a situation, practitioners have little incentive to obtain specialized training. As competition increases, however, they may view training as a means of obtaining a competitive edge. Ironically, Tseng views training as a source of both cohesion and disturbance of the market. He explains that initially, "training schools vary considerably in admission standards, duration of training, curricula and the qualifications of graduates and instructors." Training institutions may end up competing for students to stay afloat, and as a consequence, they "may oversupply the market with excessive numbers of practitioners." The increased competition makes it difficult for practitioners to convince clients "to respect their job descriptions and consequently their control over the working conditions." The result is a vicious cycle of unprofessional behavior and mistrust of practitioners by their clients (Ref. 5, p. 46).

Eventually, though, training institutions do have a positive impact, because the most highly-trained practitioners become dissatisfied with the status quo. The graduates of the most prestigious schools are likely to nurture and cultivate the same vision for the market, so that when the number of such graduates reaches a certain proportion of the practitioners in the market, the consensus that the occupation should be organized to protect clients from malpractice and themselves from outsiders comes naturally among such practitioners (Ref. 5, p. 48).

Thus begins Phase II, the consolidation of the profession and the development of a consensus about practitioners' aspirations. Training institutions must adapt to an increased demand for quality services. They also support the emergence of professional associations as a means of enhancing the prestige of their graduates. Tseng views the professional association as a critical factor in professionalization. In this third stage, professionals can really work collectively with their colleagues to exert their influence over their job description and the behavior of their collegauges, control admission into their circle and appeal to clients and the public for recognition of the profession. The power and achievements of the association strengthen the commitment of members to the course they are pursuing (Ref. 5, pp. 48-49).

The next step is for the professional association(s) to formulate ethical standards. "The enforcement of the code of ethics is crucial," Tseng points out, "because it functions externally as one of the bargaining chips to earn public trust and internally as an indispensable tool for internal control" (Ref. 5, p. 49). He also emphasizes the interdependence of the code of ethics and the professional association: As professional associations become more influential, their codes of ethics become more sophisticated and are more strictly enforced; but if enforcement is weak, the associations cannot be powerful or function properly.

Another factor in increasing professionalization is control of admission to the profession. A strong association can require all practitioners to be members in good standing in order to practice legally. It may also play a role in accreditation of practitioners, although that function is often reserved to the government. In the United States, three related professional organizations exemplify this transitional stage. On one end of the continuum is the American Translators Association, which has made accreditation a condition for active membership but has not managed to obtain any legal recognition for this status; in the middle is the court interpreting profession, represented by a number of organizations that have at best an advisory role in government-run certification programs; and at the other extreme is the Registry of Interpreters for the Deaf, which administers its own legally-recognized and enforced certification program.

As professional associations gain strength, they are able to exert more influence on the public through publicity campaigns. "With publicity measures," says Tseng, "the association tries to convince the clientele and the public to accept its definition of the professional content of work and working conditions. In other words, the purpose is to achieve market control" (Ref. 5, p. 51). If the public relations campaign is successful, the professional association can then try to influence political and legal authorities through lobbying campaigns with a view to achieving legislative recognition and licensure. This marks the final phase of Tseng's model, at which point the profession has managed to ensure its own protection and autonomy.

The transition from Phase I to Phase IV is not a smooth or quick progression, Tseng warns. "It is not a peaceful evolution, but rather a process involving conflicts and a power struggle at each stage." In particular, evolving from Phase I to Phase III depends on the resilience of the practitioners aspiring for professionalization in holding out against unqualified competitors and market encroachers. The consensus and commitment reached at the second stage are fragile, because practitioners may change their occupation if better job alternatives are available or making a living becomes too demoralizing, thus shrinking the population and reducing the force of the professional aspirants (Ref. 5, p. 53).

Tseng makes it clear that the professional association is a *sine qua non* for professionalization, but that even with an association in place, dissent among the members can weaken its effectiveness. A key factor is enforcement of the code of ethics:

> The effectiveness of the professional association in projecting the collective image of the profession to the public and legal authorities rests upon the extent to which it can control and develop the expertise and enforce the code of ethics. It is impossible to overemphasize its importance and relevance to the overall development of the profession (Ref. 5, p. 54).

Tseng stresses that professionalization is a circular process, with each phase providing feedback and reinforcement to the previous phase. It is also important to look at the social context in which an emerging profession exists, he notes. If other, more powerful professions oppose the recognition of the occupation in question as a profession, it will have a more difficult time emerging. For example, Ruth Morris (Ref. 10) has shown that the legal profession feels threatened by autonomy or independent thinking on the part of a court interpreter, fearing that the judge's role of interpreting the law and the attorney's role of presenting evidence will be usurped by the interpreter. The legal profession has tight control of the body of knowledge required for practicing law, and it will not easily relinquish that control to an allied profession. In her research, she has found negative judicial views of the interpreting process and of those who perform it, in the *traduttore traditore* tradition, spanning the gamut from annoyance to venom, with almost no understanding of the linguistic issues and dilemmas involved. Legal practitioners, whose own performance, like that of translators and interpreters, relies on the effective use and manipulation of language, were found to deny interpreters the same latitude in understanding and expressing concepts that they themselves enjoy. Thus they firmly state that, when rendering meaning from one language to another, court interpreters are not to *interpret*—this being an activity which only lawyers are to perform, but to *translate*—a term which is defined, sometimes expressly and sometimes by implication, as rendering the speaker's words verbatim.

The law continues to proscribe precisely those aspects of the interpreting process which enable it to be performed with greater accuracy because they have two undesirable side effects from the legal point of view: one is to highlight the interpreter's presence and contribution, the other is to challenge and potentially undermine the performance of the judicial participants in forensic activities (Ref. 10, p. 26).

Another factor identified by Tseng in his review of the literature on professionalization is public perception that the occupation is important and connected to the well-being of the people. ... "When a particular service of a rising profession is not in demand, the public is not likely to recognize its importance and relevance to their lives. As a result, actions taken to persuade the public to support the professionalization of a particular occupation cannot be effective" (Ref. 5, pp. 56-58).

Once again, the court interpreting profession provides a pertinent example of the role of public perception in the recognition of an occupation. Because foreigners and foreign languages are not viewed favorably in courts of law (Ref. 11), and because of the anti-immigrant, anti-criminal-defendant sentiment prevailing in many societies today, anyone associated with immigrants in the courts is regarded as undesirable. Consequently, providing qualified interpreters for litigants who do not speak English is a low priority. Morris sums up the issue uniquivocally:

> The law's denigratory attitude to foreigners, and its related distaste at having to deal with problems which arise from their presence in the host country, exclude its making proper interpreting arrangements for its dealings with them. In this way, its dire fears about defective communication become self-fulfilling (Ref. 10, pp. 28-29).

The same can be said of other areas of community interpreting, in which the interpreter is often seen as a crutch that enables an immigrant who ought to have learned English to draw public benefits of some sort.

After presenting his model of professionalization, Tseng discusses numerous obstacles to professionalization. The first one is "confusion of the professional title" (Ref. 5, p. 63). It is well known to translators and interpreters that the lay public does not understand the difference between translating and interpreting, and often misuses the terms. Furthermore, Morris (Ref. 12) has written extensively on the legal profession's attitudes toward court interpreters, and she emphasizes the need to distinguish between interpreting as an "intralingual" process that is performed by judges and that involves "determining the 'true' meaning of a written document," and the "interlingual" process involving the transfer of messages from one language to another (Ref. 10, p. 25).

Another obstacle to professionalization cited by Tseng is the lack of a systematic body of knowledge exclusive to the profession. It is a source of great frustration to translation and interpretation professionals that anyone who who has any familiarity, no matter how rudimentary, of a foreign language thinks he can interpret and translate. Thus, knowledge of languages, the basic foundation of the profession's body of knowledge (and the only aspect visible to the lay public) is not exclusively held by its practitioners. Tseng points out that little serious research has been conducted on interpreting, and there is still no consensus about whether interpreting is an art or a science (Ref. 5, p. 68). A corollary to this obstacle, then, is public misconceptions about the profession. Tseng notes that clients do not know how to recruit qualified interpreters, thereby enabling unqualified interpreters to survive in the market, provided they can maintain good relations with the clients (Ref. 5, p. 70). Paradoxically, he also points out that because of the common misconception that interpreting "is an effortless activity that can be done by any bilinguals" and that interpreters are "machines that do code-switching automatically from one language to another," clients think that it is easy to evaluate the quality of the interpreting services they are receiving. He concludes that "only when clients have no clue on which to base their evaluation of the interpretation can interpretation evoke any sense of awe among clients. This is detrimental to professionalization" (Ref. 5, pp. 70-74).

Prescriptions for Professionalization

To overcome these obstacles, Tseng advocates the development of a strong professional association that represents the majority of practitioners. He points out that an association cannot be expected to fully realize its power if it only represents a portion of competent practitioners. In a well-established profession, practitioners cannot operate without being members of a professional association. ... Therefore, the limited representation of interpreters' associations, in my opinion, is the major problem these associations are facing in the struggle to fully realize their potential (Ref. 5, p. 81).

Tseng concludes with this exhortation:

> Interpreters worldwide must join hands with researchers and scholars to develop the body of knowledge on interpretation, and in the process to settle the confusion over the professional title. Interpreters should cooperate more closely with associations they belong to in campaigns for the promotion of the profession. The associations, though they have made considerable achievements, should not degenerate into inaction because of complacency, for their objectives have not yet been reached. On the other hand, the practitioners should not be discouraged at the inherent difficulty of professionalization for interpreting, because as long as the occupation is developing and the associations adopt appropriate strategies for development, and there is the possibility of favorable changes in the overall professional climate, interpreting may have a chance of growing into maturity (Ref. 5, pp. 147-48).

Roda Roberts (Ref. 3, pp. 133-136) presents guidelines for the professionalization of community interpreting that are remarkably similar to Tseng's prescriptions, and thus lend further support to his arguments. She advocates 1) clarification of terminology (i.e., settling on a clear definition and a universally recognized name for the occupation); 2) clarification of the role(s) of the community interpreter; 3) provision of training for community interpreters; 4) provision of training for trainers of community interpreters (a very important issue that Tseng does not address); 5) provision of training for professionals working with interpreters (a more formalized version of what

Tseng terms "client education"); and 6) accreditation of community interpreters.

Tseng does not emphasize accreditation in his discussion of the conference interpreting profession in Taiwan, but he does indicate that a certification program lent more power to the interpreting profession in Australia (Ref. 5, p. 86). Roberts is a stronger advocate of accreditation:

> The respect of other professionals for community interpreters will certainly increase if the latter's competency is guaranteed by a rigorous accreditation system. Indeed, it is not enough to evaluate a potential interpreter's abilities at the end of training; what is also required is national recognition of their interpreting skills by means of an accreditation procedure established by a professional body...
> (Ref. 3, p. 136).

Morris cautions, however, that certification or accreditation alone does not guarantee professionalism (Ref. 10, p. 41).

Community Interpreting in the United States

Roberts asserts that community interpreting, though "the oldest form of interpreting in the world, has been the most neglected both by practising interpreters and by scholars" (Ref. 3, p. 127). Her description of community interpreting in general is an accurate depiction of the current situation in the United States. Whereas court interpreting is just beginning to emerge as a recognized profession in this country, albeit with obvious growing pains, other types of community interpreting are far behind. Two states, California and Washington, have attempted to implement certification programs governing certain aspects of medical interpreting, and fledgling medical interpreter associations have been founded in California, Washington, and Massachusetts.

In other institutions, such as social service agencies and school districts, Roberts' categorization of community interpreters, ranging from individuals engaged in interpreting as a full-time occupation to unpaid volunteers (Ref. 3, pp. 130-132), is apropos. In these settings, interpreting is rarely recognized as a separate occupation and is likely to be performed by employees as an adjunct to their normal duties, or in the case of languages of lesser diffusion (LLDs), by relatives of the non-

English-speaking party, including children. These ad hoc interpreters receive no training whatsoever, and are not members of any relevant professional associations. As a result, they feel no sense of commitment to interpreting as a profession.

Thus we see a vicious circle similar to that described by Tseng: Practitioners receive little recognition and low pay, and therefore have no incentive to obtain specialized training; consequently, training programs are rare and not well-funded; the low prestige and limited earning potential makes community interpreting unattractive as a career option for talented, well-educated individuals with bilingual skills. As noted above, prevailing anti-immigrant attitudes in the United States contribute to the low prestige of community interpreting. Unlike conference interpreters, whose clients are powerful leaders of the business and political worlds, community interpreters serve powerless members of society.

An added difficulty is that in many languages, there are few opportunities to work full-time as interpreters, and practitioners must engage in other occupations, such as tax preparation or real estate sales, which give them the flexibility to take occasional interpreting assignments. Because they do not specialize in interpreting, these practitioners do not have an opportunity to perfect their skills.

The market disorder described by Tseng also characterized community interpreting in the United States. Clients have no way of knowing which interpreters are competent, since there is no certification program in most areas and in most languages. Thus, they tend to accept the lowest bidder, which intensifies the competition among rival interpreters. The result is often unprofessional behavior, which further lowers the public's opinion of the occupation.

Recommendations

In conclusion, I subscribe wholeheartedly to Roberts' recommendations for the professionalization of community interpreting (Ref. 3, pp. 133-36). The practitioners of community interpreting must reach a consensus about their role and function, and must then educate their clients (both English-speaking service providers and non-English speakers). Following the sequence of steps outlined by Tseng, formal training programs should be instituted, which means that competent interpreter trainers must be identified and cultivated. As these training programs (which should be language-specific wherever possible) become established, professional associations should emerge to represent the interests of community interpreters and to enforce the code of ethics. In turn, as these associations grow stronger, they should strive to educate the public and potential clients about the role of the community interpreter and the importance of hiring a trained professional. They should also establish a good working relationship with the relevant legal authorities who may wish to regulate the profession. A credible certification program should be developed to encourage practitioners to obtain proper training and to instill public trust in the profession. As Tseng noted, this is not a linear process, but a circular or spiral progression, with each stage influencing both the preceding and succeeding ones.

As a result of this process, community interpreting will be a strong and respected profession with a recognized body of knowledge and credentialing process, a financially and intellectually rewarding occupation that will attract the most qualified practitioners. It will not be a smooth or easy process, but it will be well worth the effort.

References

1. Gonzalez, Roseann, Victoria Vazquez, and Holly Mikkelson. *Fundamentals of Court Interpreting: Theory, Policy, and Practice*. Durham, NC: Carolina Academic Press, 1991.
2. Unattributed article, "Community interpreting: Affirmation of a new discipline" in *Language International* 7.4 (1995), pp. 14-15.
3. Roberts, Roda. "Community Interpreting Today and Tomorrow," in Peter Krawutschke, ed. *Proceedings of the 35th Annual Conference of the American Translators Association*. Medford, NJ: Learned Information, 1994, pp. 127-138.
4. Carr, Sylvana, Roda Roberts, Aideen Dufour, and Dini Steyn. *The critical link: Interpreters in the community. Papers from the 1st International Conference on Interpreting in Legal, Health, and Social Service Settings, Geneva Park, Canada, June 1-4, 1995*. Amsterdam, Philadelphia: John Benjamins Publishing, forthcoming.
5. Tseng, Joseph. *Interpreting as an Emerging Profession in Taiwan — A Sociological Model*. Unpublished Master's Thesis, Fu Jen Catholic University, Taiwan, 1992.
6. Carter, M.J. and others. "Occupation to Profession Continuum—Status and Future of AAHPERD," *Journal of Physical Education, Recreation and Dance*, 61(3), 106-09, cited in Tseng, op. cit.
7. Mellinkoff, David. *The Language of the Law*. Boston, Toronto: Little, Brown & Co. 1963.
8. Freidson, E. *Professional Powers: A Study of the Institutionalization of Formal Knowledge*. Chicago: University of Chicago Press, 1986, cited in Tseng, op. cit.
9. Wilding, P. *Professional Power and Social Welfare*, Routledge & Kegan Paul Ltd., 1982, cited in Tseng, op. cit.
10. Morris, Ruth, "The Moral Dilemmas of Court Interpreting." *The Translator*, Vol. 1, No. 1, 1995, pp. 25-46.
11. Morris, Ruth, "Pragmatism, Precept and Passions: The Attitudes of English-Language Legal Systems to Non-English Speakers" in Marshall Morris, ed. *Translation and the Law*. Amsterdam, Philadelphia: John Benjamins Publishing, 1995, pp. 263-79.
12. Morris, Ruth. *Images of the Interpreter: A Study of Language-Switching in the Legal Process*. Ph.D. thesis, Lancaster University: Department of Law, 1993.

Notes

Notes